DISPERSALS

ALSO BY JESSICA J. LEE

Two Trees Make a Forest

Turning

DISPERSALS

On **Plants, Borders,**
and **Belonging**

Jessica J. Lee

Catapult New York

First Catapult edition: 2024

Grateful acknowledgment for reprinting materials is made to the following: Excerpt from "Ladders, Trees, Complexity, and Other Metaphors in Evolutionary Thinking" © 2017 by Andreas Hejnol, from *Arts of Living on a Damaged Planet: Ghosts*, eds. Anna Tsing, Heather Swanson, Elaine Gan, and Nils Bubandt, reproduced with permission of the publisher. Excerpt from "Tofu Heart" © 2020 by Nina Mingya Powles, from *Vittles*, reproduced with permission of the author. Excerpt from *Small Bodies of Water* © 2021 by Nina Mingya Powles, reproduced with permission of the author. Excerpt from *The Ecology of Invasions by Animals and Plants* © 2020 by Charles Elton, reproduced with permission of the licensor through PLSclear. Excerpt from "Versatile and Cheap" © 2013 by Ines Prodöhl, from *Journal of Global History* 8, reproduced with permission. Excerpt from V. S. Naipaul, "Jasmine," *The Times Literary Supplement*, June 4, 1964, reproduced with permission of the publisher.

"Border Trees," "Sweetness," "Tidal," "Words for Tea," "Bitter Greens," "Bean," and "Synonyms for 'Mauve'" are based upon articles first published in the *Catapult* column Non-Native Species.

ISBN: 978-1-64622-178-3

Library of Congress Control Number: 2023943190

Jacket design by Nicole Caputo
Jacket art: willow herb © iStock / Inna Sinano; roots © iStock / brainmaster; elderberry © iStock / cat_arch_angel; tansy © Michel Viard/Horizon Features / Bridgeman Images
Book design by tracy danes

Catapult
New York, NY
books.catapult.co

Printed in the United States of America
10 9 8 7 6 5 4 3 2 1

CONTENTS

A Note to the Reader

WHAT HAPPENS WHEN A PLANT—OR A PEOPLE— moves from one place to another? We often turn to language to offer a frame. So we have introduced species, invasives, exotics, and weeds. So we have "plant immigrants." Or indeed, too often when applied to people, just "migrants."

I became preoccupied with this question in 2018, as I wrote of local species I'd met high in the Taiwanese Central Mountain Range, only to learn later that these species, when encountered elsewhere, are considered highly invasive. I'd seen trees whose closest genetic relatives were spread wide across the world, and I began to wonder whether all these plants deserved a bit more thought than I was accustomed to giving them. I'd been in Taiwan examining my own family's migration story. The parallels felt insistent, if imperfect.

When I was a child, my paternal grandmother had a

painted window hanging of a European robin. Beneath it sat a suncatcher. When the light shone through, it refracted into beams of colour that danced upon the kitchen walls. The essays in this collection are rather like that: in each, plants illuminate facets of life and our world—whether personal, political, ecological, scientific, or otherwise. The plants, here, are displaced in a range of ways: some are seen as weeds hitching a ride around the globe, some are valuable crops humans have intentionally extracted from one place to another, while others are cultural artefacts of human stewardship or technoscientific plant breeding. These stories are but a fraction of their being in the world. As I wrote, I came to see more clearly that the trees, shrubs, grasses, mosses, algae, and seeds in this book are forces of their own, making worlds far beyond my imagination and interpretation. Our pictures of the world are only ever fragmentary. Our language for plants is much the same.

In *Arts of Living on a Damaged Planet*, the biologist Andreas Hejnol writes that "Metaphors are always a double bind: they at once allow us to see and stop up our abilities to notice." So while I offer the frame of "plants out of place," the essays here do not always offer answers. As neither an ecologist nor a horticulturalist but a historian, I dwell upon the question of how some of our many ideas about plants and place have been formed. I examine the stories that constellate around species we've encountered through our own migrations around the globe. And as a writer, I ask whether these ideas might serve us any longer.

These essays were written during a period of personal upheaval: between the very beginning of the COVID-19 pandemic and the end of 2022, a time during which my family lived in four different homes, in three cities, across two countries. None of these moves were predicted far in advance, so as I examined plants uprooted from their homes, I felt more adrift than ever. The personal timelines in this book are thus fragmentary; like the plants considered, my own story is told in movement. I began writing these pieces in Berlin, continued them in London, then in Cambridge, and then, unexpectedly, once more again in Berlin. I became a mother in this time, felt my own relations to the world cleave open and rearrange themselves. The pieces very roughly track these seasons of life. And like seasons, their timelines loop and loop again.

As I write this note to you, the cold season is upon us. Thick snow has covered much of England, and Germany gets rain for Christmas. The birch trees on my street still hold their yellow leaves.

These are essays written for a world in motion. Plants that, in dispersal, might teach us what it means to live in the wake of change.

DISPERSALS

I.

Margin

MARGIN, 2021

It is April, midmorning on a Wednesday, and I have come to the pond alone. Three months I've been away from this water, quiet in my apartment. I am no longer inured to the cold, so when I step down the ladder I hesitate. Cold pools around my ankles, and then my feet disappear into black. The pond is clear, a sign that the sediment that normally hangs in the water has settled. Filling my throat with air, I lower myself in and turn towards the distance. As I swim out, I veer into the shallows: beneath the willow, where my legs brush shoreline weeds. I feel my feet tangle. And just for a moment, I am breathless.

At the edge of the water, there is a spray of reeds. In springtime they've not yet reached their full height, growth still slowed by lingering cold. But they are collecting themselves, readying leaves and buds and shoots to unfurl. These are marginal plants. Those grown at the edge of the water, at the border between land and lake. Theirs is a territory blurred and impermanent, contracting with heavy rains, starved of life with summer droughts. I watch the margins as I swim.

To speak of margins is to speak of edges, of borders. A word that tastes of paper, but also of place. Three generations of my family have lived as migrants. Each with very different fortunes: My maternal grandparents lost their first homes to a civil war and gave up their second with the narrow hope of new opportunity. My paternal grandparents migrated late in life, to be closer to family. My mother and my father met when both were new to Canada—and then there is my sister and me. We wear a border in our bodies. My sister, strangers often point out, looks so much like my Taiwanese mother, and I, like my Welsh father. My sister has stayed in the town we grew up in, and I have not stopped moving. I have made and left homes every few years. Always learning somehow to begin anew.

Plants that grow on the edge between two kinds of environments are asked to be agile: to belong not just to a world of water, but to dry land as well. There are other beings, too, that have this agility: Those we've uprooted and carried across global currents. Those we class as other to the place in which they find themselves.

Plants are often considered static. The word we often use to describe them, "rooted," is also how we might describe our human belonging to a place. But when I think of seed, of blossom, root, and rhizome, it is *movement* that I think of.

So what does it mean to be a plant out of place?

The pond is not, in its most literal sense, a natural place. It is anthropogenic. Once a stream of the River Fleet, the pond was dug as one in a chain of reservoirs around the early seventeenth century. A pile of clay, puddled to a hard surface, used as a source of drinking water. And now, it is the picture of a rural idyll. A pond made, a landscape planted: the trees here were added mostly in the 1920s and '30s. Oak, hawthorn, alder. Sycamore, holly, and yew. And in the past few years, the margins of this pond have been re-created. Dug up to restore drainage, relaid, and re-planted with native plants. Reeds, lilies, and loosestrife. It is a place designed and maintained to look the way it does. Picturesque. When I swim here, I find myself in an ideal-ised vision of the English landscape. Careful, cultivated, intentional.

Scientifically speaking, the native plants here belong to a "temperate pond habitat." But in my mind, they also be-long to a more human frame: that of culture and of country.

LAKE EFFECT, 1994

It is my mother who teaches me about longing.

The route to Moore Water Gardens took us nearly to Lake Erie, skirting the creek that flowed through the nearby town. The shop sold plants, fish, snails, and stones, all burbling in little above-ground ponds dotted around the site. But going to Moore's is an event I associate mostly with trees: with the wall of green that lined the highway, robinia, spruce, ailanthus, and pine. Somewhere along the road, near a break in the green, stood a chip wagon, plywood peeling, where we'd buy butterscotch milkshakes and skin-on fries after my mother had filled the car with plants and koi bobbing in clear plastic bags. The smell of waterweed in the air, the slick of oil and salt on my fingers.

My parents both immigrated to Canada in the 1970s. They aligned themselves with society's expectations of immigrants: they were hardworking; they built a prosperous life for themselves and our family. My father likes to tell us how he came with only twenty dollars and no education. He does not say that he came with whiteness, or masculinity, or with fluent English on his tongue. My mother came with none of these. So on balance you might say they started with little. By the time I was two, we moved to a four-bedroom house in the suburbs, with a backyard that stretched a hundred feet into pine woodland. I say this because it feels important to say: my parents contorted themselves into the shape of success, whatever that might be. But my mother longed acutely for a past way of living.

Her longing began indoors, in a room we called the Chinese Room. She filled this room with objects picked up back in Taiwan. Jade-inlaid screens and a collection of snuff bottles. Lacquered furniture and ornate scrolls. Then, sometime in the early 1990s, her longing wound its way outside. What started as a tiny pond grew to the size of a small swimming pool: at first, an oblong no more than a metre across, cut from the turf in our suburban yard. My mother strewed rocks around the edge, ran a pipe up a mound of stone to create a waterfall. The rubber pond liner gave the water an inky hue, brightened only by the pale petals of flowers bought from Moore's. Pink and white waterlilies, perched atop the surface like ascending stars. Mauve hyacinths, puckered with yellow at their centres, and a velvet froth of duckweed. My mother, in an effort to compose their exact position in the pond, would climb right into the water, moving their pots, weighing each plant down with pebbles. In ornate Chinese urns she'd bargained for in Chinatown and carefully positioned around the back deck and pond, she planted paper reeds and irises, floated water lettuce in between.

The plants gathered a wider world into our pond: Paper reeds are native to the Nile Delta, where they are now virtually extinct. But they thrive where they have been introduced as ornamentals, their range expanding as our planet warms. Water lettuce is not native to the hemisphere where we lived but spread by human action to nearly every waterway of our world. Both, depending on where you find them, are considered invasive. Both have been spread by our hands.

The pond echoed of other places. But in our suburban backyard in London, Ontario, my mother created something she knew as home.

Winters in Canada's Snow Belt are cold, with snowstorms building as the weather moves over the warmth of the Great Lakes. This is what's known as the Lake Effect. Each winter was wrapped with snow. Our pond was too shallow for the fish to remain outside, so every October, before the cold set in, my family would crowd outdoors with white plastic buckets and green nets. We'd scoop each koi into a bucket of pond water, and one by one they'd be transferred indoors, where we kept a two-metre-long tank in the dining room. Pursing her lips around a clear plastic tube, my mother would suck the pond water from the buckets into the aquarium, moving the carefully crafted outdoor habitat indoors. And so each winter I would spend time watching the fish behind glass—learning each of their patternings, their mannerisms, their habits. I'd watch them bob near the side of the tank, polishing algae from its mirror surface. I wondered what they made of this glassy world, in a bright-lit house with white tile everywhere. If they missed the green of outdoors, the muck of the pond's bottom.

When I was twelve, my parents divorced. My mother moved to an apartment across town, taking her Chinese urns with her. The pond and the koi, being confined to the backyard, remained with my father. But by now the fish had outgrown the small pond. They were too big to overwinter in the tank indoors. So he hired a contractor to dig out a lower, larger pond. The dig took weeks, soil eked out by hand. Piles of earth built up around the garden, eventually to be covered over with stones and shrubs.

This new pond was deeper than the last, so the fish could remain at its bottom come the cold. One Saturday, Dad and I drove to the TSC farm store on the west side of town and bought a cattle trough heater. After that, the water stayed warm through winter. My mother's fish no longer did their annual migration.

WATERWAY, 2012

The water always had the cut of stone to it: cold, slick, a deep black. Light would reach only so far, refracting into copper rays when it reached the green growing up from the bottom. The Severn River, where it flowed past the cottage, felt more to me like a lake: currentless and often still as glass. An enclosed thing, though you could in fact travel more than three hundred kilometres along it. I swam there thinking of it as a place unto itself. But the waterweeds told another story.

It was May, the first weekend up at my stepmother's cottage each year, when we scoured the site for damage wrought by winter. Displaced decking and clogged-up pipes. That year, we'd had to pull up the water pipe that ran beneath the dock to the house. Which meant mucking out weeds along a shallow stretch of the shoreline. No one else would go in the water at that time of year—it barely registered eleven degrees after the recent snowmelt—so, inured to cold, I was sent in.

Skin prickling, I struggled to submerge a rake in an effort to unmat the weeds grown over the water pipe. The deeper I moved, the more impossible it became, so I began reaching out with my hands. Coils of green life, frilly and soft, twined around them. I uprooted a frond and examined it, each leaf spread to form a tidy whorl. European water milfoil—considered one of the worst invasives in the region, except perhaps zebra mussels—grew in dense clusters in these shallows.

Noxious, nonnative, invasive. They hardly seemed like the right words for a plant so delicate to look at. But these words shaped how I looked at it nonetheless. European water milfoil has a profound ecological impact, crowding out native milfoil species and thus damaging invertebrate habitats reliant on them. Quite how the plant—native to Europe, Asia, and Northern Africa—got to be in a waterway in central Ontario remains unclear. Early studies suggest it arrived in ballast waters in the 1940s, while phylogeographers have proposed its arrival via shipping from Asia through the 1960s. It was and remains a problem in the region.

It needed to come out, I knew that much. Left to grow as it willed, the shallows here could turn dark and hypoxic, and the pipes and motors we relied on could clog. It slumped into a mess of green when I placed it on dry land, but when I submerged it again the milfoil unfurled, delicate and fine. I pulled piles up from the riverbed, and we added them to our fire. But I couldn't help admiring its beauty: I longed to see it in its native range, where it grew *in place*, where I could meet the milfoil without thinking mostly of its harm.

MUSEUM, 2013

The ponds in front of the National Palace Museum were cut through with paths, stones slick with winter rain. We bobbed umbrellas above our heads, peering over the edges of the bridge to catch a glimpse of the life below. Koi, orange and white. And lotuses, pads dappling the grey with green. That day, my mother took more interest in the gardens than the museum itself, glancing past artefacts in glass cases and rushing us outside. Because this garden made her feel something. A kind of longing, perhaps, or belonging. Can a garden offer a sense of identity? A sense of self in the arrangement of pond and path, plant and person? My mother seemed to think so.

"It is *traditional*," she kept saying. "So tranquil, so composed." I thought then of the pond my mother had built when I was child, and of the Chinese Room, and all the small ways she'd tried to bring Taiwan into our house in the suburbs.

Was this the thing she had wanted? The garden at the

museum was designed to reflect Sung and Ming dynasty Chinese gardening styles: pavilions and bridges over irregularly shaped ponds, a landscape unfurling like a poem. Our little backyard could never achieve the scale needed, the ability to meander, the possibility of a garden unfolding itself like a map as you moved through it. But I could see this garden's traces in our own: the way a stone was placed, the way a plant was positioned. The tiny details that kept my mother anchored to her home. The things she used to root elsewhere.

That was why, as soon as my mother had another home and another garden, she unpacked her urns and filled them with plants. She dug another pond and framed the views towards it with a miniature páifang gate and a broad pergola. She cleaned the pond each summer by wading into it, green twining around her limbs. In time her koi learned to recognise her footsteps at the same time each day, crowding at the surface of the water for their food. She'd feed them from her hands, submerging her arm just enough that it blurred into the body of water.

ECLIPSE, 2021

It is June, and the water has warmed to slick comfort. The weather isn't especially nice today, but still there are so many women here. It's a Thursday morning, and I've come out in that blurry time between morning and noon, breaking my day with a swim.

Today is an eclipse day. I should be at my desk, but I wanted to watch the sky from the water. So in the minutes before the moon passes between the Earth and its sun, I swim out into the pond. It is busy, all the women swimming clockwise towards the far end, and then back along the meadow bank. Pale clouds pattern the sky. As the shadow of the eclipse passes—taking a small bite from the midsummer daylight—I swim along. Watching the women swimming with their backs towards the sun. The summer blooms spraying into the edges of the meadow. The coots and moorhens and mandarin ducks bobbing at the dock in hopes of the lifeguards' food.

Even in the pond, borders become unruly. Crocosmia—with its spray of crimson flowers and slick green leaves—grows downstream of here. It is a common garden plant, native to South Africa, but the U.K. Wildlife and Countryside Act lists it as invasive in the wild. One pond down in the chain, in the fenced-in edges of the bird sanctuary, grows giant hogweed, likely the most recognisable invasive species in the country. Here where the margins have been carefully planted with British plants, other species are uprooted and controlled.

Land managers hope that through the planting of reeds and marginal plants like water mint, the pond will become a better kind of habitat: a place with broader margins, a better nesting place for grass snakes and the great crested newt, a vulnerable protected species across Europe. The plants that dwell here may not be showy—to many, they may simply be a blur of brown and green at the edge of the water—but they are essential. Without these margins, the pond cannot accommodate all who seek a home here.

LAKE, 2018

Paddling from our camp in the corner of Brandenburg, we emerged from a narrow, tree-sheltered stream to a wider, more windswept lake. Small choppy waves rose here, nudging our canoes in rhythm as we cut our way westward. I'd paddled this lake plateau of Germany many times— swum it even more often—but still I was enlivened by the sights made possible by being in the middle of the water. Away from dry land, away from the roads and trails that only loosely strung themselves around this region. Water was a way of seeing more—at a different angle, below the land and roots of trees that forest east Germany. Here I could see freshwater life clearly. White and butter-yellow lilies bobbing in our gentle wake. Lotus seed heads plump and patterned with holes—these only ever sent my mind wandering to food, to chilli-flecked lotus root salads and sweet soups scattered with lotus seeds. Beneath us, sago pondweed danced like fennel fronds strung underwater. Every so often, my oar would bring up a strand of it and I'd twizzle its stems between my fingers. Jade green and delicate.

But I learned later that this plant was hardier than it

appeared—as happy to grow in still lakes as it is in rivers, canals, ditches, and brackish lagoons. In turbid conditions, aquatic plants like sago pondweed help a body of water return to a period of relative clarity and health. In the late 1980s, when one of this region's largest lakes began to recover from eutrophication, sago pondweed was one of the first species to slowly recolonise the lake and thrive, having survived even when the water was depleted of oxygen.

A map of sago pondweed's native range shows nearly the entire planet; it lives on every continent except Antarctica. I look at the list of countries it calls home, a paragraph-size blot of places from Afghanistan to Zimbabwe, and a purple highlight over Hawai'i, the only place it is considered introduced. Sago pondweed's range is therefore described as "cosmopolitan."

What is it to be a world citizen amongst species? The sago pondweed lives under a banner of free movement in a world increasingly marked by borders. But the natural world presses against our tendency to lay arbitrary geopolitical boundaries upon it—and we, by our own movements, likewise transgress the borders we apply.

The first time I contemplated what it meant to be cosmopolitan, I was eighteen, clutching a pink pocket-size book by Jacques Derrida. To speak of the cosmopolitan, I read, requires us to speak of hospitality. A posture of welcome from those who stay in place.

For those who move, the realities of movement are far different. The first international standard for passports was not agreed upon until the 1920s, in the aftermath of the First World War. Efforts at plant quarantine, however, preceded it by decades. Measures to control the movement of plants across borders were widely enacted in the late nineteenth and early twentieth centuries, with national legislation on pest control and quarantines coming into effect in Britain, the United States, Canada, France, Germany, and the Netherlands, amongst others, as knowledge of plant pests and the means of controlling them increased. But what of the world that does not fall tidily within these maps? Not all passports grant the same rights of passage. Some species—like the pondweed—might belong everywhere at once.

Though I move, just as my parents and grandparents have, I do not want to live afloat, at home anywhere I go. My friends are buying houses, asking which of my phone numbers is still valid and which they can delete. I am in movement nonetheless. Each time I move I find myself longing for a past place, unable to wash it from me. I am my mother's daughter, seeking ponds in every place.

When I read of the sago pondweed's recolonisation of that Berlin lake, I learn that it spread itself not by seed, but through tubers reaching beneath the lakebed, slow and persistent. What would it mean to move and stay rooted—to have roots that can span continents?

In conservation, the term "charismatic megafauna" refers to those animals that have widespread appeal to humans, that might capture the care and imagination of the broader public. These are the animals we see in charity appeals: tigers, elephants, pandas, polar bears. It is on their backs that the conservation of a habitat may be seen to rest.

In a 2018 study listing the twenty most charismatic species, there are none that live in freshwater. There are no sturgeon or catfish in conservation drives, despite a third of freshwater fish species currently facing extinction. Still less is said of the plants that live in these habitats: water violets and marsh club moss and creeping marshwort and many others.

For a time, I take my swims in the River Cam. At Grantchester there is a ladder that moves, plonked into the riverbed by a loosely affiliated group of swimmers who sometimes bring toolkits to the riverbank, banging in stray nails on the ladder's steps, replacing rusty hinges. Sometimes they replace the ladder altogether—for some months there is a metal painter's ladder, and for many more a wooden step ladder. Each week I find it somewhere else along a twenty-metre stretch of scalloped bank, tucked into the soil amidst a spray of nettles and marginal plants. Sometimes, when the water level fluctuates along this floodplain, I cannot find it at all.

On lucky days, I swim with my neighbour Becky at

the Riverbank Club, where there are much more reliable ladders into the deep. This stretch of the Cam is narrow, lined on either side with retaining walls and shaded by heavy green growth. In spring, volunteers plant a meadow of wildflowers around each ladder, so that lowering myself into the water becomes an act of descending into colour.

Swimming here, I cannot avoid thinking of the health of the river. Every few months, a news article reports on the state of sewage outflows into the Cam. A local swimmers' group updates one another about discharges on rainy days, marking out on a map the safest places to take their swims. Upriver, conservationists have begun pouring gravel and adding fencing to create new cattle drinks along the water, hoping to preserve what marginal plants remain on the banks. They remove Himalayan balsam from the banks and over the course of many years prior have removed rafts of the invasive North American species floating pennywort from the water. Downriver and across Jesus Green, the city proposes to transform a freshwater ditch into a "new wetland area." Replacing a concrete bank with wetland plants seems desirable—until it is noted that endangered water voles are nesting behind the bank. The margins prove more complicated than the city planners want to admit.

It is high summer when I steal an hour from the day to venture down to Hodson's Folly. A pair of biology students are hosting a botanical swim, offering what they say is the first and only botanical swimmer certification. They've printed out certificates for all who attend, a flourish of clip art and a gold seal to make it official. It is the hottest day of the year so far—thirty-two degrees—and at least twenty swimmers have turned up.

We plunge out into the river, avoiding the punts that crowd past and the teens that dive from the nearby bridge. Swimming along the bank, we learn the species of the riparian zone up close—the dogwoods that make up the riverbank's undergrowth and the willows that lean out over them. Yellow irises line one part of the opposite bank. One by one, we hold up whatever weeds tangle around our limbs, and the leaders identify them. Treading water, they name what grows nearby: arrowhead and marsh marigold, loosestrife and water mint. And tape grass. This species, they tell us, is not native to Britain and with the impacts of climate change *could* become a problematic invasive. But for now, it does other things: Here, the tape grass helps secure the riverbank's integrity, reaching into the sediment and even increasing dissolved oxygen. Elsewhere, they say, tape grass is often used for erosion control. So what ought we to make of its presence here? I thread a strand through my fingers, feeling the heft of its green life weightless in the water. And I do not have an answer.

Paddling back towards the stone bank, I am reminded of my mother—the way she would climb into her backyard pond, the way she dropped her ankles into puddles to catch minnows and tadpoles when I was a child. My mother's freshwater idyll looked nothing like this stone folly built by a nineteenth-century father so that his daughters could safely swim. But still, I think she might love this place. That each stretch of river, pond, lake from which I swim somehow brings me to Moore's, to the taste of salt and butterscotch, to the smell of pondweed and the glint of fish scales. To a beauty my mother longed to re-create for herself. My mother found charisma in the margins, and it is from her that I learned to love.

2.

Border Trees

BERLIN IS A CITY OF STONE ON SAND. COBBLES cross the pavements at irregular angles. Grey, russet, pewter, brown. Once carved through with concrete: haphazard and hastily erected, a hundred miles of dull border wall and fence. Unrenovated Altbau apartments are a peculiar shade of greige—the colour of dust and soil and sticky smoke. And for much of the year, the skies are the same. Silver and unsaturated. But I came to associate Berlin instead with a particular shade of pink: fuchsia sunsets, the ripple of cherry through white ice cream. Spring in the city was coloured with flirtation, like bubble gum or confetti. Clouds of blossoms covered the trees.

My first home in the city, an aging apartment on a corner by Bernauer Straße U-Bahn, reminded me of the film *The Lives of Others*. The landlord, an American artist, had furnished it with vintage East German furniture and left the rooms unrenovated. Floorboards wobbled and plaster peeled (an easy shorthand for "creative" in this city), and a balcony overlooked the path where the Wall once stood. The day I moved in, the landlord showed me to the cellar—where people once dug escape tunnels, he added, as if it were a selling point—and gestured towards the storage unit that came with the apartment. I couldn't stop staring at the walls, the sections where brick and mortar had been patched. I never went into the cellar again.

In those first months living in the city, I was meant to be writing. More often, I took to walking and cycling along the Wall's route. Partly because it was there. But in some sense, because I wanted to tell myself I was paying attention to *History*. I didn't want to be someone who moved to the city for the nightlife—not that one couldn't. I felt I owed the place some solemnity.

The Mauerweg (Wall Trail) traverses the old borders of the city, tracking along forest roads, city streets, and the depths of lakes. Near home, where the death strip had not yet filled with new apartments, birch and ailanthus grew scrappy and lean. I picked through these trees on my way to the shops, ambling for coffees and flowers and takeaways. On the city's edges, where the Wall cut into suburbs, plantation pines stood skinny and green.

In the city, plaques mark the Wall's old course. In lakes, I swam across it, marvelling at where an edge had once been written in water. The Mauerweg is a space that could—and in some ways should—devastate us. But in spring, I learned, it is also the ground from which the cherry trees grow.

Upon the fall of the Wall in 1989, ten thousand cherry trees in total were gifted to the city by a donation campaign led by Japanese television station TV Asahi. They were planted in the symbolic space left by the Wall: blossoms meant to unify a severed city once again. Following suit, other streets in the city were planted with cherries. They line the streets of my old Kiez, grow in our last apartment's courtyard, and pepper the lawns of local parks. In spring, along some of the most visited sections of the Wall, luminescent flowers cluster on the trees, calling locals from the grey weight of winter.

Six springtimes passed with me living there; my life in that time became more joyous than I could have imagined. Walking amongst the cherries was a particular pleasure. Each year, I wanted to drink in their colour and beauty, as if I could carry it through the year. Unimaginably light, they seemed frivolous even, in a city where so much once felt too heavy to hold.

I speak of the cherry blossom, but it is the rose that gives its name to their botanical family: the Rosaceae. The family tends towards showiness, and many of its plants are known for their flowers and fruits. Rose, rowan, raspberry. Hawthorns and meadowsweet. Species in the Rosaceae are amongst the most economically and aesthetically valued in our world. Apples, almonds, apricots. Plums, peaches, and pears. And in the family's genus *Prunus*, there is the cherry—both fruiting varieties and those grown for their flowers. Cherries are trees whose histories can be captured in movement: the fruiting European cultivars were brought to North America by settler-colonists, and the hardy North American timber cherries went in the opposite direction. That the ornamentals are often called by their Japanese name—sakura—speaks of a similar transience. These are trees that have travelled.

A sakura might be one of many types: some four hundred varieties have been cultivated from wild mountain species originating in China, Korea, and Japan. Because accurately tracing the lineages of these cherries and their nomenclature has historically been complicated, cultivated ornamental varieties have more often been classed simply as Sato-zakura, "village cherries." Though exact names have been hard to pin down, commonly the trees planted along city streets might be varieties of *Prunus serrulata*, renowned for its frilly flowers; *Prunus pseudocerasus*, with flat, cheerful blooms; *Prunus × subhirtella*, a winter bloomer; or the most commonly planted Somei-Yoshino (*Prunus × yedoensis*) cherries, with their delicate pink-white petals.

Perhaps because of their short blossoming season, which was easy to miss entirely, these flowering cherries were largely overlooked in favour of more edible *Prunus* species when first encountered by Western travellers on plant-collecting missions in the eighteenth century. Samples of the ornamental trees had been sent to botanical societies in the West as early as the beginning of the nineteenth century, but it wasn't until nearly a hundred years later that the trees became well-known there. But once encountered, they inspired exalted prose from European travellers to Japan, China, and Korea. The *Prunus serrulata* was, in the words of nineteenth-century botanist John Lindley, "one of the most ornamental hardy plants with which I am acquainted." Robert Fortune—the Scottish plant collector who made his name gathering plants across East Asia—described the double-blossomed cherries as "the most beautiful objects, loaded . . . with flowers as large as little roses" and marvelled at the way their petals fell "like thin flakes of snow." Recounting a visit to Japan in 1907, Marie Stopes—a British suffragette, scientist, and eugenicist—wrote of blossoms "like great clouds touched rosy by the setting sun" and which felt "like whipped-cream when you kissed them." Collingwood Ingram, a British plant collector famed for collecting and restoring threatened varieties of cherry, described the trees as "superlatively lovely," with "a refined charm, when in bloom, and a delicacy of colour and form that appeal to one's aesthetic sense in a way that the others can never do."

But despite this novelty in the West, the sakura has long been central to Japanese culture. So much so that an 1893 handbook for young Japanese botanists explained tree anatomy with reference only to the sakura, its leaves, roots, and branches as the prototypical Japanese tree. The trees invite festivals in their honour, with such celebrations speaking to the cherry's role in centuries-old agrarian cosmology: a healthy and well-timed flowering signalled a good rice crop each year. After the eighth century, when the imperial family began hosting annual celebrations of blossoming trees, hanami (flower viewing) grew in popularity amongst urban dwellers, with many composing and reciting poetry about the ephemeral beauty of the blossoms. This springtime practice has, over the matter of centuries, become synonymous with viewing cherry blossoms specifically, "the queen/king of flowers in Japanese," though it had once included a range of other blooms.

By the late nineteenth century and the turn of the twentieth, Japan had won the First Sino-Japanese War, and neighbouring Taiwan fell under its claim. Korea, by 1905, came under occupation, too. And as Japan was annexing territory in surrounding lands—acts of colonisation not unlike those of the West—it cultivated relationships with European and North American powers. The gifting of sakura trees became a vital component of Japanese diplomacy. In 1909, American travel writer Eliza Scidmore, who'd long been enamoured of cherry blossoms, suggested to First Lady Helen Taft that the trees be planted in Washington, D.C. During a visit by William Howard Taft and his wife to Japan two years earlier, the blossoms had caught Helen's eye, so she quickly took up Scidmore's suggestion and made arrangements with the Japanese embassy. After much diplomatic wrangling—including an initial shipment of some two thousand trees in the winter of 1909 that were, just a month after their arrival, deemed so infested with pests that they needed to be burned—the plan was in motion. Japan's gift to the American nation, a second shipment of trees courtesy of the City of Tokyo, arrived in 1912. Altogether, three thousand cherry trees were planted along the Tidal Basin and Potomac River in Washington, D.C., that year—a gift of friendship. The White House sent dogwoods in return.

These gifts of trees have graced the cities I've called home: In 1959, Toronto was presented with two thousand Somei-Yoshino trees, in a project led by first-generation Japanese Canadians and the Japanese consulate. In 2019 in London, the first trees from a gift of more than six thousand cherry trees were planted in several of the Royal Parks, with the rest to be planted across the country. The thousands that grow in the former border strip in Berlin are but a few amongst the many trees that have been cultivated, packaged, and sailed or flown across the globe in the name of friendship and diplomacy.

But the cherry blossom's symbolism is not altogether straightforward. Though for many centuries the sakura had been associated with vitality, towards the end of the nineteenth century, falling cherry petals became associated with precisely the opposite: death. "The master trope of Japan's imperial nationalism," writes anthropologist Emiko Ohnuki-Tierney, is the phrase "'You shall die like beautiful falling cherry petals for the emperor.'"

As the Japanese empire expanded, so, too, did the dark ideals of the sakura. The late-nineteenth-century philosopher and militarist Nishi Amane explicitly positioned the cherry blossom in opposition to the peony and rose of Sharon—emblems of China and Korea, respectively—noting that cherry blossoms had the good decency to fall from the tree before decaying. Nishi's thinking was vital in shaping the foundations of the Imperial Army. To him the blossoms came to stand in for virtue and the superior qualities of the nation and its people. By the Second Sino-Japanese War and the Second World War, this association between the cherry blossom and empire was cemented: Japanese planes were painted with the emblem of a single cherry blossom. Women waved pilots off with blooming branches, and tokkōtai pilots (kamikaze) flew to their deaths with sakura pinned to their breasts.

And the cherry blossom was not merely deployed as symbol: actual trees were planted across occupied territories like Korea and Taiwan, and existing cherry trees were sought out and maintained. It was an intervention in the landscape intended to turn colonised land into Japanese land, and thereby inspire the same transformation in people. So Japanese varieties of cherries were planted amidst native king cherry trees in Korea. In 1995, fifty years after Japan's surrender in the Second World War, cherries planted by the Japanese were cut down at Seoul's Gyeongbok Palace. The legacy of colonisation remains symbolically and intimately linked with the cherries, even as they continue to be celebrated for their beauty.

In Taiwan, where *Prunus campanulata* is native, Somei-Yoshino trees were planted in the cities, across the grounds of shrines and temples. But the seasons in Taiwan do not match those of Japan. Being markedly warmer, the blossoms arrive as early as late January or mid-February, often in time with the Spring Festival or Lunar New Year.

In the decades after Japan's surrender of Taiwan to Chinese Nationalists—another set of colonists—my family would find themselves amidst these trees. At the border between winter and spring, my mother and her parents, and nearly everyone in Taipei it seemed, would venture into Yangmingshan to watch them bloom. My mother's childhood was not entirely happy, but this memory stands out. They rarely spent time together as a family—my grandfather lived hours away for his work in the air force—but on the annual trip to see the cherry blossoms, my mother had both her parents by her side. My grandfather carried her on his shoulders. To her, the cherry blossoms meant only lightness, love. She did not think of blossoms falling, or anything of death.

The mobilisation of nature in service of imperialism and nationalism is by no means isolated to Japan: The environmental historian Alfred Crosby famously argued that the age of exploration not only brought "new-world" plants like potatoes, tomatoes, and tobacco back to Europe, but also was followed by the planting of European flora across newly colonised terrain. Scots pine, dandelions, and English ivy all came to North America via Europe, while in India the introduction of nonnative species has been traced back to the British East India Company's botanical gardens. Where colonies were established, plants that reminded the colonisers of home usually followed.

Through mythmaking and symbolism, the natural world comes to stand in for potent human ideals: the sakura as an embodiment of Japanese faithfulness to the emperor, the oak as a symbol of enduring Englishness. The bald eagle signifies freedom for U.S. Americans, but in Germany, the eagle remains a problematic image: the Reichsadler (Imperial Eagle) had been deployed as a symbol of power since the late nineteenth century, but today it carries the stain of its history as a Nazi symbol and continued use by neo-Nazis. The two eagles are distinct: the original Reichsadler, still used in an updated design to this day, depicts an eagle with graceful, arced wings. The Nazi symbol, by contrast, shows a rigid eagle stood atop a swastika, its wings stretched hard against the horizon. It was, and remains, a message of hate.

That nonhuman nature—from blossoms to birds—remains fraught with the baggage of human history seems to me somehow unfair. It seems, at best, to centre human narratives in a world far more complex than us. But this is a world we've irrevocably transformed; little in the work of transplanting and introducing species across the globe seems guided by fairness, and I know my tendency to think in such terms is naive. Lauret Savoy writes in her exquisite memoir *Trace* that human attempts to order nature arose from a "colonial world trade that collected human beings as it collected exotic plants and animals." In the wake of human actions, the trees remind us there is no neutral nature, no blank wilderness. Still, I wonder how these symbols we've made might reply to the stories we tell about them.

In cherry blossoms, scientists now find something more vital and potent than these prior imaginings. As our world warms, the sakura stands as sentinel for anthropogenic climate change.

At Tokyo's Yasukuni Shrine, dedicated to fallen soldiers of the empire, one cherry tree represents all its kin. The Yasukuni Index Tree, a decades-old Somei-Yoshino, is used to measure the beginning and zenith of the cherry blossom season. But one tree cannot account for all the changes in our world. So since at least the 1930s, Japanese scientists have been collating data on cherry blossom festivals: when historic festivals fell offers a unique insight into temperature changes over time. And accounts of Japanese cherry blossom festivals go back much further than usual datasets on flowering trees: abundant records stretch back to the fifteenth and sixteenth centuries—with some reaching back to the ninth century. The records follow the period when the cherries were markers of the agricultural year, a symbol of vitality and romance, and the decades in which they took on the darker sheen of nationalism. In centuries-old diaries and court records, the traces of a cooler climate remain.

The data show that cherries have typically bloomed over a six-week range from late March to early May. Much as the timing of the blossoms historically portended fruitful or dire harvests, these trees of the past offer us a stark warning. By the 1980s and 1990s, the cherries began consistently flowering earlier than at any other time over the past 1,200 years.

In Berlin, in December 2019, in the months before the world would find itself indoors, I was often outside. The temperature most days hovered well above freezing. It was the second winter in a row I'd left my parka packed in a vacuum-sealed bag under the bed; the second without snow. The trees replied. Autumn-flowering cherries in my local park blossomed more fully than I'd ever seen before. A year earlier, I'd read about cherry trees in Japan that had blossomed in October, a trick of the temperature after a year of extreme weather. I couldn't stop thinking of the strangeness of their colour in autumn. The trees in my park kept their blooms through the holidays: for ten winter weeks in total. The flowers were smaller than those of springtime—the size of a quarter—but fully formed, the petals tightly stacked and luminescent. Instead of snow, pale petals dusted the ground in January.

When the cherries bloomed again in March, the pandemic was upon us. Wearing masks and sunglasses, my husband and I strolled with our dog beneath the cherries along the path of the Wall. We marvelled at their pinks against the grey. This was a land marked by loss. The trees stretched their roots beneath it and scattered the path with petals, indifferent perhaps. That spring, it seemed wondrous to me that cherry blossoms could hold the weight of histories laid upon them, even briefly, before the flowers fell again.

3.

Frontier

A PORTRAIT OF THE EXPLORER

Enter the explorer. His ship is built of oak and elm, with masts of pine and fir. His ship is made of steel. His ship is called *Endeavour. Pizarro. Utowana.* And he hails from London. Berlin. A town in Kansas.

Enter the explorer. He carries with him a notebook. A knife. One hundred pounds of paper. He carries with him a Wardian case. Carries with him an army. His ship lands shy of Tahiti. Venezuela. Malabo.

Here is an explorer, and his name will be recorded.

A VISION OF THE WORLD

When I was four, my father built a bookshelf in the basement, oak on a dark-green wall. Neither of my parents are readers, but my dad was a lover of geography, so he filled the shelf with maps. Maps were introduced early in my childhood, because he wanted my sister and me to learn to read them. My mother did not understand them, however many times he tried to teach her. So from an early age he taught us cardinal directions, how to use a compass, how to use an atlas. He kept them in the glove box and the back seat of the car. Kept a pre-aged globe, designed to look authentic. Pressed the seams of every map to ensure it was folded correctly.

On the bookshelf he stored his atlases and folded sheets, photo essays, and travelogues. The remainder of the shelves was for biographies and how-to guides—for business acumen, social success—and a decade's worth of magazines.

While I was still learning to read, *National Geographic* was my portal to another world, because I could spend my time looking at the pictures, tracing my fingers over the words I knew. My father didn't like it when I pulled maps from the shelf without supervision—I had a habit of folding them up wrong, bunching the wrong sides of the paper together in frustration—but I was free to look through the magazines. So I pulled each from the shelf in turn, every yellow spine revealing a new glossy vision of a world I'd not yet seen. Silver-grey dolphins poised in a shallow sea. A rendered image of dinosaurs, though I could not understand at the time that it was not a photograph. A refugee girl with green eyes—my father always talked about how this was the best cover, the most exquisite photograph he'd ever seen. Everyone seemed to think so, though it would be decades before anyone learned her name.

I spent more time looking at the advertisements than anything else. Half- and full-page spreads every few pages, with colour images of Ford pick-up trucks and Pontiacs. There was always a page devoted to Dramamine near the back, and an image of a compass watch that every man needed. In every issue, an advert for a camera—Kodak or Olympus. And so I learned the essential requirements of an adventurer. To know directions and to tell the time. To know how to document the world in image. Motion sickness would be a problem for me: I'd been suffering sea sickness since childhood, could not ride in a train seat backwards, could not glance out a car window to look behind. But with the right tablets, *National Geographic* taught me, anything might be possible.

In *The Poetics of Space*, Gaston Bachelard writes of the basement of the home as a space of irrational dreaming: a space of the unconscious, a space of inward darkness. I do not think this is entirely right: in those years I went to the basement to dream of a wider world. I dreamt of sunlight and of other lands, a world that was bound in yellow.

A PORTRAIT OF THE EXPLORER

The first time I learn about David Fairchild, it is in a description of a contemporary explorer. He is compared to eighteenth-century adventurer-scientists like Alexander von Humboldt. He is compared to Joseph Banks, to Robert Fortune. Fairchild is described alongside plant collectors who transformed not just the study of botany, but also through their plant introductions transformed ecosystems. He is compared to those who carried out their collecting as a form of espionage. But Fairchild didn't begin life that way—and in the course of his life, I think, it is possible to see the potency of these ideas take hold: of what it means to be an explorer, of what it means to cast distant lands into otherness.

David Fairchild was born in 1869, a century after Humboldt. The era of exploration preceded him; he was born an American in the height of the age of empire. When he was ten, his family moved from Michigan to Kansas. And there he lived in a land where winter snow would drift indoors, where in spring, the dust from farm fields would rush over everything. Fairchild grew up around plants: his father was in charge of the state agricultural college, a connection that would lead him to study botany himself and work, at first, studying plant diseases on behalf of the fledging U.S. Department of Agriculture. He would study botany in Naples, Breslau, and Berlin. Until, under the wing of his patron, Barbour Lathrop, he leaves everything behind to explore Java.

Portraits of Fairchild present a straitlaced scientist who quietens his longing for a wider world through work. But when he meets Lathrop—a chance encounter with the philanthropist and world traveller—he is asked to state his deepest dreams: to visit Java, to understand plants and their pathologies in place. Lathrop finds Fairchild's interest in the details of science dull, and asks him whether he'd better enjoy collecting plants from across the world. American agriculture doesn't yet have much beyond staple crops like wheat, maize, oats, or potatoes. Novelty, Lathrop reasons, could be of value. It is in this interaction that the future of U.S. agriculture and ecology is transformed.

Lathrop offers to finance Fairchild's travels. But the young botanist does not feel ready. He wants to study further, to prime himself for the adventure Lathrop invites him to undertake. So Fairchild, by dream or by circumstance, learns to embody the role of the explorer. On a first collecting mission on behalf of the United States—seeking cuttings of the Corsican citron—he finds himself carrying out his work in secret. It is, in his words, an "ill-fated expedition from the start," as he ventures through Corsica wary of bandits, only to find once he is already there that the secretary of the USDA refuses to officially authorise his mission. "But there I was, with an adventure on my hands," he writes in his biography. He counts the coins in his pocket, decides to carry on, is nearly arrested once, and eventually sources the cuttings from a roadside grove. He sticks them into slices of raw potato to keep them alive and sends the citron back to the United States by post.

In 1896, Lathrop takes him to Java at last, and it is

there that Fairchild encounters fruits he has never seen up close: mangosteens, durian, coconuts, pomelos, and rambutans. Wearing white trousers, white shirts, pith helmets, and satchels, he and Lathrop begin to realise a dream of introducing new plants to the United States. But the dream of plant introduction first requires plant extraction. He packs seeds in paraffin, seeds in dry charcoal.

Fairchild is no longer a plant pathologist content with study. He has seen more of the world now and is reticent to stop. In the winter of 1897 to 1898, with twenty thousand dollars from the American government, Fairchild and the botanist Walter T. Swingle establish the USDA's Section of Foreign Seed and Plant Introduction. They build a station in south Florida, with Fairchild set to direct its operations, bringing plants from across the globe for the benefit of American agriculture. But this job is largely administrative. At the urging of Lathrop, Fairchild immediately turns away from the bureaucracy this work entails. He asks permission instead to become a "special agent" travelling the world in search of plants, carrying out the work of his new office in the field. Permission is granted.

Over the coming years, Fairchild will travel the world by boat. The *Utowana* is designed expressly for collection and extraction. It has "a well-lighted laboratory for microscopical work; a delightfully arranged library with desks and bookshelves; a dark room; a special device for drying seeds and specimens; a deck to hold Wardian cases on and ample storage spaces for supplies of all sorts." On these missions, Fairchild will be responsible for the introduction of hundreds of thousands of seeds or plants. And the term "special agent" quickly gives way to a more explanatory— but equally evocative—title: "agricultural explorer."

Fairchild led the USDA's plant introduction efforts for three decades. Their work was carried out by a clutch of specialist explorers: Frank Meyer, who travelled more than a thousand miles along Marco Polo's routes, eventually lending his name to the Meyer lemon. Palemon Howard Dorsett, who made more than five thousand accessions of soybeans to USDA collections. Walter Swingle, the father of Florida citrus. Frederick Wilson Popenoe, who travelled South America and brought back avocados. One of the founding missions of the USDA was "to procure, propagate, and distribute among the people new and valuable seeds and plants." Knowledge of foreign plants, the contemporary historian Tiago Saraiva notes, was essential for cultivation and settlement across the varied ecologies of the American landscape. It was the explorers, in part, who made it possible. The plants they brought back, in USDA vernacular, were called "plant immigrants." And Fairchild signed off department circulars with the title "Agricultural Explorer in Charge."

Now, I watch silent films of Fairchild's explorers from the National Agricultural Library. In each of them, the botanists resemble an archetype: their clothes are bright, clean; their postures upright. Locals chew betel, climb trees barefoot, raise bamboo huts. The self-styling of these botanists as adventurers is plain. The captions are written by Fairchild himself. In one, I read: "On a trek of 250 miles through the jungles of Achin the explorers found many species of unfamiliar plants, made many photographs and secured a wealth of plant material. The escort of soldiers, provided by the Governor, assisted in collecting plant material." In another film, atop a globe centred on Asia, the captions speak of wayfaring, enterprising voyagers: "Under the blazing sun of the tropics—On the windswept plains of the North—the intrepid explorers brave man, beast and climate in search for new plants."

Fairchild's autobiography reveals a man who becomes drawn to extremes: early in the book, he writes that he considered abandoning science altogether. In one scene he is asking to be ordained as a monk in the hills beyond Naples, seeking an ascetic life. Pages later, he longs to sail to Java, to live a life of exploration away from the plains of Kansas. The dream he has is potent.

A VISION OF THE WORLD

When I am ten, my father takes me to the mall, to get a passport photograph at Blacks. The back is stamped and dated, and he affixes the photograph to a form, a paperclip at the corner. My birth certificate, a folded yellow-beige card, and his are tucked behind. This will secure my passage, he tells me, to so much of the world.

In a few months' time, my British passport arrives, burgundy-bound. My father slides it into the black cabinet next to my blue Canadian passport, but not before I flip through every page, tracing their purple-pink swirls. I am a child, so I do not understand what this passport grants me. My father explains that it is not just a passport to his home country. It is a passport to Europe. And that, he tells me, is a kind of freedom. He tells me that when I am older, I can live and work almost anywhere I choose. That I am lucky to have this, because most of my friends will not. I do not know at the time that he is speaking of a future that will materialise: that I will use this passport more than any other. That I will be living in Europe under the rights it grants on the day those rights become fewer.

Then, I am still a child. My ideas of adventure are more modest than moving abroad: I become a teenager and decide I want to learn to rock climb. I want to buy a mountain bike. There is a boy named Dan who tells me about a trail ride between home and school, asks if I want to bike it one day after class. I am desperate to seem like the kind of girl who rides a mountain bike. Who is not at all afraid.

When I have the TV to myself, I turn to channel 44, to OLN. It was called the Outdoor Life Network before, but they recently rebranded, so the channel seems cooler. I watch a travel show where a group of backpackers takes turns hosting, leading the camera down back alleys on their gap years abroad. The title credits are a pastiche of fonts, an electric guitar distorted to let us know the show is alternative. Between episodes, there is an ident where a man snowboards from the top of a snow-thick cliff. On MuchMusic, I hope I'll catch a music video in which a white man asks how it feels to be alive. There is an image of him skydiving. Rock climbing. Scuba diving. Swimming with dolphins. I add these things to the mental list of what adventure looks like. It's not a problem that I'm afraid of deep water. That I'm afraid of heights. That I am a mixed-race girl in the suburbs.

In all the visions I see, I learn it's important to set out alone. It won't be until adulthood that I read of the labours behind exploration: of local scouts, translators, field guides. As a teenager I read about men who climb Everest, but I do not learn the names of the Sherpas. Adventure, I think, is a solo act.

A PORTRAIT OF THE EXPLORER

It is 2018 when I read an obituary of Yamei Kin, who died in 1934. The obituary is published by *The New York Times* as part of a series rectifying the paper's longstanding focus on white men.

The portrait is of a woman more formidable than any other of her time. The first Chinese woman to earn a medical degree from an American college. The leader of a laboratory at the USDA tasked with introducing soybeans to the American diet. Soybean cheese, the article says: a food we better know as tofu.

In 1917, off the back of First World War food shortages, the USDA sent Yamei Kin to China as an agricultural explorer. She was to gather methods of soy production, alongside other plant explorers gathering seed. A full-page spread in *The New York Times Magazine* was devoted to her mission. An etching of Kin, dressed in Chinese clothes, a book open on her lap, topped the page. Her expression is unreadable.

Born in China in 1864, Kin was orphaned before being adopted by American missionaries who raised her abroad. By the time she reached adulthood and got her degree—under the Anglicised name Y. May King—she was better poised than many to elaborate the benefits of a Chinese diet across the cultural divide. In her work for the USDA, she demonstrated methods for fermenting soybeans, for creating soy sauce, tofu, miso, and more. She moved seamlessly between her cultural knowledge of China and her American self. But this act of translation—her methods for turning tofu into chocolate pudding to please American palates—is not all that interests me about her.

Kin was the first woman I encountered when I began to learn about the USDA's plant collection. She was, I read, a woman who left her deadbeat husband and was legally divorced in absentia on grounds of desertion. She was a woman who loved travelling alone, calling herself a widow. A woman who was celebrated for her expertise, who gave lectures across the country and abroad. A woman who brought soybeans to the West but never as a plant extracted from the culture that created it. She never chose between places or peoples.

In everything I read, Kin was a woman who lived in two worlds. She navigated the masculine, scientific realm of American plant exploration. And she was born and died at home in China—on a farm she bought for herself, on the land beyond Beijing.

A VISION OF THE WORLD

By the time I reach university, my desire to see the world is coupled with a knowledge that the kinds of exploration I have read about no longer exist. At our shared student house, my friends and I decorate with maps of places we'd like to visit. My flatmate brings home a collection of vintage *National Geographic* magazines from a yard sale down the road, and we spend our university years with stacks of yellow lining our corridor.

Wanting to do something that changes the world, I decide my humanities degree should be a double major with international development. I imagine myself working in conservation, working with NGOs. In one group project, we're asked to generate a sustainable development idea complete with risk assessments, business plans, and ethics forms. We are nineteen and know little of how best to help the wider world. So we propose an idea we can imagine working: an ecotourism project in Brazil. We download photographs of the exact forest where it would take place. Complete ethics assessments on working with locals. Design brochures and decide how profits will be funnelled back into local projects.

That same term, a professor assigns us a chapter from Edward Said's *Orientalism*. It is the first time I've encountered the word "Orient" against its other: "Occident." It is the first time I've thought about what "Oriental" might mean aside from the uses I've always known: As the word my father uses to describe my mother—never "Chinese," never "Taiwanese." As the word my mother uses to describe her culture when she complains about life in the West.

I read of the ways in which the idea of the Orient is not simply a fantasy of otherness, of foreign lands and cultures. It is an idea enacted through institutions, through modes of power that continually recast the West as neutral, powerful, a point of origin. And the Orient—from China to the Mediterranean—as a frontier.

At nineteen, I am not yet ready to imagine the ways this language applies to a person like me—a person made by both.

A PORTRAIT OF THE EXPLORER

David Fairchild retired from the USDA in 1935. By the end of his career, agricultural explorers had introduced eighty thousand accessions to the USDA's collections. A biography of him lists a fraction of the plants for whose introduction he can be credited: "citrons, mangoes, sour citrus, hardy avocados, spineless cactus, seedless grapes, pummelos, hops, hazelnuts, grapes, carob, walnuts, olives, lemons, dates, pistachios, blood oranges, almonds, peaches, persimmons, litchis, plums, mangosteens, loquats, bamboo, pineapples, jujubes, and even . . . flowering cherry trees." Stories of his life trade in many of the same descriptions: He is intrepid. An adventurer. A botanical spy. He has sought the frontier and brought back its riches.

Today, internal histories of the USDA's Office of Seed and Plant Introduction are at pains to argue that things have changed. The department now goes by a confounding name, the USDA Agricultural Research Service's National Germplasm Resources Laboratory's Plant Exchange Office, or the PEO for short. The work of science is foregrounded, the days of intrepid adventure behind them. No longer is plant collection a realm of botanists swashbuckling across the world. Scientists and seed curators are sent on missions approved through channels of bureaucracy. There is paperwork—much more than there once was—and a Code of Conduct. Since the 1993 Convention on Biological Diversity and subsequent guidelines for international plant exchange, missions must be conducted in partnership with host countries. Despite this, I encounter an echo: these journeys are still called plant exploration.

Of course, the USDA's agricultural explorers were not—and are not—alone in their collecting. Today, in the rebranded Kew collection programme in Madagascar—run by the Millennium Seed Bank Partnership based in Sussex, England—seeds are gathered in collaboration with researchers and institutions overseas. Kew researchers train those on the ground to replicate their practices far away, out in the field. There remains a home base of plant exploration. The field—the frontier—remains foreign.

I do not bemoan the end of the era or the bureaucracy designed to create accountability in a field that was, and remains, deeply entwined with its imperial origins. And I admit to finding a thrill in the stories of Fairchild and his counterparts—to finding an evocative joy in their lists of fruits grown in thick tropical heat, in the language of their botany, even if I am troubled by the power men held in this era, by their privilege. But I am also troubled by the value ascribed to a plant extracted—from a foreign land, a foreign people, and the cultures of knowledge that belong with them. If their histories demonstrate anything to me, it is that there is power in the language we use to describe these explorations.

There is a power, too, in the plants that have been collected—and most of all, in who holds them. In 2000, the Botanical Garden of New York began to repatriate plant specimen data that had been collected in Mexico to the Mexican biodiversity database. Since 2010, digital records of plants have been repatriated to a Brazilian archive from Kew, from Harvard, from a herbarium in Stockholm, and more than seventy other collections. Small seed banks are restoring species to the Indigenous communities that stewarded them into existence. Plant collection leaves a living legacy. In seeds, specimens, and the knowledge they produce.

A VISION OF THE WORLD

I didn't pursue a grand career in international development in the end—I left the programme uneasy at the idea. That was the running joke amongst students: if you finished your IDS degree, you'd never do it for a living.

Instead, in my work writing and studying histories of place, I found an uneasy beauty in the archives. In etchings from von Humboldt's travels. In the records of botanists who named so much of the living world. And those, like the agricultural explorers, who brought plants back. I travel most widely in the words they left on the page.

When we graduated, my flatmates and I held a yard sale. We stacked up all the magazines we owned—*Vogue* and *Martha Stewart Living* and *Real Simple*, all dog-eared and tea-stained. We sold each for fifty cents apiece, surprised at how much we could earn.

But the *National Geographic* magazines drew a special kind of interest. Other students flipped through the issues, perhaps struck by how vividly the pictures brought back their own childhood dreaming. Their ideas of what it meant, in youth, to venture out into the world.

One neighbour was particularly keen. Maybe he had dreams of adventure. Or was just an art student, hoping to use them for collage. I cannot say. But he bought the lot at a dollar each. He carried them home in batches, yellow spines heavy in his arms. Where the magazines had once stood in our hallway, there remained an outline in dust.

4.

Sweetness

WHEN I WAS NINE, TWO DECADES AFTER ARRIV-
ing in Canada with almost nothing, my parents turned the
hard corner into wealth. They'd worked all hours for as long
as I could remember, building their home renovations business from door-to-door sales to owning their own factory
in the course of my short lifetime. It was a feat I could
not understand then. I did not know what it meant for my
father—a tool-and-die maker's son from a family of coal
miners—to have left school at sixteen and ventured across
the world alone. For my mother, newly arrived from Taiwan, to have met my father and learned his Welsh-accented
English as they built their lives together.

To celebrate, they bought a second home: a condo-
minium on the Gulf Coast of Florida. It had a mango tree
in the backyard. From then on, they eschewed the option
of visiting their home countries and decided that we would

spend every school holiday and summer vacation at the condo. I asked my father if having a second home meant we were rich, but he replied simply that it was inappropriate to talk about money and went back to his work, which he carried ceaselessly between our homes.

Each day we spent in Florida, my father sat at his desk, still working. Seeking entertainment, I turned my attention instead to the riches I could find outdoors. I learned new rhythms. Summer afternoons on the coast broke into thunderstorms at 3:00 p.m. like clockwork. The condo was on a small, mostly residential island with a building height restriction. It was safe enough for me to spend an entire day outside, making friends with neighbourhood kids. I learned to ride bikes to the Circle K for Cherry Coke and how to shuffle my feet on the seabed to avoid stingrays. With American friends, I learned to exchange words like "garbage" for "trash," "pop" for "soda." They asked if we had penguins in Canada. They asked why my sister and I didn't look how they expected Canadians to look.

In the backyard, I helped my mother with the gardening. The weather in Florida reminded her of Taiwan: lush growth, heat, humidity. The air was tactile, ambrosial. Behind the condo, the mango tree stood three storeys tall, flinging leaf into every spare corner of light.

I cannot say how old it was, nor what variety of mango it yielded, but I remember every detail of the shade it cast. I remember the feel of its bark, the weight of its fruit. The ground around it had a sap-sweet smell from overripe drupes that fell and returned to the soil.

A few days every summer, my mother would draw an extendable pole out of the garage. At its end were a bag and blade, fastened to a string and a trigger. When the fruit came in full and ripe, she leaned from the balcony, reaching each pink drupe with her picking pole. She pulled the trigger, and the mangoes fell into the canvas bag with a heavy thud. One by one, I transferred them to a white plastic basin for my mother to rinse and eat in the afternoons and evenings. She mostly ate them alone; I was picky.

It was on one of those days that I learned the Mandarin word for "mango," 芒果 (mángguǒ), and that the word for "fruit," 果, is also the word for "result" or "consequence."

Mangifera indica L. carries its origins in its botanical name; the mango has historically been understood to come from India, from the foothills of the Himalayas. The *L* stands for "Linnaeus," the Swedish botanist who classified the plant based on samples sent to him, but who may never have actually seen a mango tree for himself.

Domesticated some four thousand years ago, it is amongst the earliest fruit species in the region to fall under human care and cultivation: its entry into our human use spans as far back as peaches, as oranges, as lemons. But exactly when and where this domestication took place remains disputed. Though conventional wisdom has pointed to its domestication solely in India, more recent genetic analysis has suggested that the mango was plucked from the wild multiple times, domesticated in multiple places spanning India and Southeast Asia.

Like cashews, sumac, and pistachios, the mango belongs to the Anacardiaceae family, most notable for its irritant plants, poison ivy and poison oak. When I studied botany during my PhD, our instructor gave us stern warnings about the Anacardiaceae: we should learn to recognise the family by smell (crushed or slashed parts of these plants smell, conveniently, of mangoes) and, should we ever find ourselves doing field research, to handle the sap with care. A picture of rash-inflamed skin flashed up on the instructor's PowerPoint under the words "Sap—Beware!!"

The lessons proved valuable: though I hadn't eaten them as a child, I grew up to learn that I have a mild but rare allergy to mangoes, which means that if I ingest their skin or sap, I end up with hives and itching skin for days afterwards. It isn't an exact science; sometimes I break out, and sometimes I don't. So now I eat mangoes rarely and only in circumstances where I can control their preparation. But despite this—perhaps because eating them is such a rare thing for me—I long for the sweetness of their juice, the redolent smell of that mango tree from childhood.

Mangoes—revered and prized by almost every culture

in which they are cultivated—are a migrant fruit. I mean this in the obvious way: the story of the fruit speaks of plants spread through human migration from India, Burma, and the Malay Peninsula to China, perhaps by Buddhist monks in the fourth or fifth centuries; by Persian traders to East Africa by the tenth, and the Philippines by the fifteenth. Thereafter, its movements mirror colonisation. Mangoes were cultivated nearly anywhere the trees would survive, from Hawai'i to West Africa, spread especially along routes traversed by Spanish and Portuguese colonists and through French and English botanical gardens. The mango travelled to Brazil, to the Caribbean, and ultimately to continental North America. Though hundreds of cultivars have been recorded worldwide, today, most commercial varieties of mangoes were developed in Florida. With human help, mangoes circumnavigated the globe.

Introduced to Florida in 1833—and with more varieties brought over in the early decades of the twentieth century by USDA explorers tasked with combing the world for novel species—the mango came to preoccupy local plant breeders. How could they make a mango that would travel well and thrive in large plantations? Now, these Floridian mangoes dominate what we find in supermarkets across Europe and North America: cultivars like Tommy Atkins—with mottled ruby skin and a bland flavour—or Kent, deemed reliable but not exceptional, and Keitt, green and heavy, all "preferred by the market." They grow across the world, fed into commodity chains in place of tastier, sweeter, more fragrant types maligned as "ethnic varieties" for ethnic communities. These other mangoes, not bred for commercial monoculture, ironically do not travel as well.

This story is contained in language, too. Across all the languages I speak, the word for mango is a loanword: "mango" in English, Spanish, and German, "mangue" in French, 芒果 (mángguǒ) in Mandarin. Its name has stayed relatively the same in almost every place it appears. "Mango" comes from the Portuguese "manga," which comes from Malay, and ultimately from the Malayalam "മാങ്ങ" (maanga). Portugal held colonies in India as early as 1505. That we say "mango" is a trace of this legacy.

But to speak of migration, language, and the mango is more complicated than it appears.

The mango can be an uneasy symbol for many: like the coconut, it is often a crude, performative shorthand for tropical places. In E. M. Forster's 1924 novel *A Passage to India*, mangoes are almost obsessively discussed. They are the orientalised objects on which stories hang, the currency with which to treat a guest: "'But what can we offer to detain them?' 'Mangoes, mangoes.'" They are the fruit that make it possible to "make India in England," just as England was made by colonists in India. In Forster's hands, the notion that mangoes signify bounty becomes an agonising thing. In one famous passage, they are likened to a woman's chest: "'For you I shall arrange a lady with breasts like mangoes.'"

In the middle of the twentieth century, by contrast, for writers from newly independent former colonies, mentioning mangoes, guavas, plantains, or breadfruit lent legitimacy to a natural world that had, under colonialism, been sidelined against the ideal of European nature reified in literature. In a 1964 essay entitled "Jasmine," V. S. Naipaul describes a passage of text in which women were likened to all manner of Trinidadian flora, not pejoratively, but as a reclamation. "Fiction or any work of the imagination, whatever its quality," he writes, "hallows its subject."

By the end of the century, however, the fate of fruit had shifted once more. The mango had become so ubiquitous as to be deemed cliché. Critics pointed to the opening lines of Arundhati Roy's 1997 novel *The God of Small Things*, where "black crows gorge on bright mangoes" and to a wave of "sari-and-mango novels" that followed it. As if exiling the fruit from fiction, the writer Jeet Thayil proclaimed in a 2012 radio segment, "I try to avoid any mention of mangoes, of spices and monsoons."

In a matter of decades, fruit had become extraordinarily fraught, and mangoes, in particular, had the unfortunate tendency of signifying exoticism performed for a white gaze.

But when I began to write this essay—deep in the dullness of a quarantined springtime—I started asking friends about mangoes. The replies I received told me something vaster than the trite cliché of sensual sweetness. A Filipina living in Germany told me of the small, candy-like fruit she missed from childhood; I learned that the Philippines are famous for having the best mangoes in the world. I learned of aunts and uncles who posted boxes of Alphonso mangoes across the world for relatives in the United States to eat, clustered around the dining table, all at once. A Chinese Malaysian Pākehā friend told me she had been taught by her Indo Swiss friend how best to eat the fruit. I heard how the Swedish American daughter of a California rancher taught every visitor how best to slice the fruit.

I read of campaigns against a 2014 mango ban on Indian imports to the European Union, sparked by fears of infestation by invasive fruit flies. The ban decimated sales of Alphonsos that year, suspending the annual rituals of the mango season for the South Asian diaspora in the United Kingdom. These stories weren't about some tropical Other, but about the traces of a past—of skill and familiarity—that remained after migration.

A more recent wave of essays reflects this sentiment. Dianne Jacob, in her 2016 essay "The Meaning of Mangoes," writes of the time her father—an Iraqi Jew from Shanghai who'd immigrated to Vancouver—imported a box of mangoes, which he left to ripen in the basement.

The air became a "fragrant cloud of tropical musk," and the mangoes came to signify a kind of forbidden pleasure. The Japanese American cartoonist Sam Nakahira writes of her grandparents' Hawaiian mango tree, its fruit's unparalleled sweetness, and her fear that in time, these mangoes will simply become memories. K-Ming Chang, in an essay called "Consequences of Water," writes of mangoes, kumquats, guavas, and her Taiwanese mother. In her words, fruit and the body are intertwined, and the act of cutting fruit is an inherited, familial memory. Here, mangoes are swelled with sweetness, with water, and with rain. Mangoes signify more than nostalgia. They stand in quite literally for the self and for home.

Gathering all these words, I called my mother.

Here I, too, will resort to cliché, like Proust and his madeleine dipped in tea. I am fascinated by the way words can be bound tight to past places, by the way a simple question can unfold an entire scene, long thought forgotten. The way a fruit—even just its mention—can carry more than its weight in flesh.

I asked my mother about the mango tree in our garden. My parents divorced some years after they'd bought the condo in Florida, and in the decades after, my mother had mentioned more than a few times how much she missed that tree and its fruit. "I remember you saying how much you loved them during childhood," I added. I could not have expected the story she told me then; she remembered it only in the moment of my asking.

In the summer of 1960, my grandmother and my mother were living in a rented room in the countryside outside Taipei. My grandfather, an air force colonel, lived on an airbase two hours away in Taiwan's south. My mother was six years old and spent her time roaming the rice paddies nearby or catching butterflies in the garden.

One evening, on the way home from her work as a secretary for the Nationalist government in Taipei, my grandmother stopped at the fruit market. She bought five kilograms of mangoes—the tiny, yellow-green Taiwanese variety. As the sun set, with an enamel basin at their feet, my mother and her mother sat silent on low wooden stools beneath the trellis of the garden. My grandmother carefully peeled each mango for my mother, who sucked the sugar-sweet fruits clean to their pits. Warm juice dripped from her chin but also from her hands, her arms. It dripped from her elbows to the dust on the ground.

"This was," my mother told me over the phone, "one of my happiest memories."

I didn't know how to reply.

To say that my mother's relationship with my grandmother was strained would be putting it delicately. I had heard so many stories from her past and arranged them accordingly: stories of love and beauty featured my grand-father; the violent, painful ones involved my grandmother. There are some stories that are not mine to share.

But this was the first happy memory I had heard about my grandmother. The first time my mother had painted the scene for me: that countryside home, the garden, the warmth. I thanked her for telling me; she thanked me, too, for asking.

My mother didn't say anything else; it sufficed, per-haps, to have told me this much. A lifetime later, it was the mango—brimming with more than sweetness—that she was left with.

5.

Tidal

AT WALPOLE BAY, MIST POURS IN FROM THE North Sea. My feet, then my legs and body disappear into grey. I've never swum here in sun—I prefer the rain anyway—but still I'm caught off guard. Not by the cold nor the depth, but by the tangle in which I immediately find myself. Halfway along the tidal pool, where waves heave up over the rock wall, slicks of kelp slide over my legs and across my torso.

Porcelain crabs, stony and brown, dapple the shoreline. Daubs of seafoam pulse where the chalk reef creeps onto land, and the rocks are furred with algae and red weeds. This is a zone of transition, where the tide fills the space between land and sea. Salt water and life suspended.

I kick my legs from the kelp and propel forward into the waves, salt stinging at my lips. I hear my dog whining on the shore, waves pooling around his paws as he watches me disappear into the sea. It is his first time on the beach, and having never seen waves before, he skips away as they rush towards shore. He hates it when I swim.

When I pull myself back onto land, I stumble. There isn't any clear ground for us to stand on, with the beach blanketed in weeds spent by the winter tide. The smells of rot and salt have accumulated, and each new wave lumps more seaweeds onto the shoreline. But the dog is relieved, lapping at the salt water on my legs as I dress. I've returned to him with new scents, with prickled, icy skin.

No one else is coming to the beach today. It is only just April and bitterly cold. Britain is held tight by travel restrictions, and we are unable to leave the land we stand on. But the wrack and brown kelp still move—thriving amidst the chalk reef of the shoreline. I lift a frond of kelp with the toe of my boot, letting its length twine around me, and imagine its journey to shore. For seaweeds move wherever the sea—or we—might take them.

"Algae," as a term, is a broad brushstroke: it gestures towards the difficult, unclassified things that live in the otherworld of water. Taking in some fifty thousand species in fresh and salt water, they span taxonomic kingdoms—from bacteria to the not-quite-plant, single- and multi-cellular organisms—and depending on where you live, these classifications themselves can shift. Much of this is down to size: we don't often speak of algae in the singular—as alga—and we find it hard to relate to species we can hardly see. But seaweeds like kelp and wrack—the macroalgae of the world—capture our attention more readily.

Some twelve thousand species of seaweed have been recorded, and it is likely you'll be familiar with a few of them. They are the algae we eat: dulse, wakame, kombu. Or like bladder wrack, a source of iodine in medicines. *Porphyra* algae is processed to become the nori used in sushi or to make Welsh laverbread. Algae pervades even our land-bound lives: as fertiliser and farm fodder, largely unseen, but also in other, more intimate ways. If you brushed your teeth today, your toothpaste may have contained seaweed as a gelling agent. Seaweed products are in everything from paper to pharmaceuticals to fuels. And in this shape-shifting space, they come to mean so much to humans: sustenance, familiarity, otherness, and futurity.

As a child, I was no lover of seaweeds. They were weeds after all, with the unwanted tendency to drift out of place. No matter that in my Taiwanese mother's language they were sea vegetables (海菜 | hǎicài), a term more resonant of sustenance. I saw them only as things of another world, things that brushed at my legs as I swam, that evoked a rising terror.

I was fearful, and the same fear of seaweed I had while swimming carried over onto land. At the dinner table, I pushed away stray pieces of kombu, picked it out of stir-fries, and turned up my nose at nori. I couldn't bring myself to eat the tofu-and-seaweed salads my sister loved or my mother's sparerib soups strewn with kelp. For a long time, seaweed felt to me too redolent of the sea: tasting faintly of fish and brine. My Welsh grandparents and father spoke of laverbread: a seaweed puree made of boiled *Porphyra* algae. I couldn't understand wanting to eat it; the thought of its squidge between my teeth turned my stomach. I knew I was being picky, that my mother loved these foods and wanted me to as well. But I was more accustomed to the crunch of North American snacks. I wanted Lunchables pizza and Ritz crackers. I struggled with the foods everyone else in my family seemed to love.

Then, one day, I'm eleven, on the other side of the country from the rest of my family. I'm with strangers, a mother and daughter near my age—a homestay weekend during a month-long summer camp. They're doing everything they can to make me feel at home. They take me for ice cream down the end of the street where they live in Vancouver and offer me toast with lemon curd every morning once they realise how much I like it. This Saturday, a grey day despite it being summer, they've taken me crabbing.

I don't eat seafood, but I want to be polite. I think I might find crabbing fun, anyway, as we get to go out on a little tin boat with their friend, a gruff man in a puffy vest. The sound of boat bells hangs in the air, and the clouds sit low in the sky. We clip orange life vests over our bodies and pile into the little Stanley, minding our feet around stray tools that clutter the floor: buckets and crab traps, ropes and gloves, all sloshing in the remains of a recent rainfall.

We spend a while out on the boat, tossing traps and hauling them back again, checking to see what we've caught. But we aren't very successful—and to tell the truth I don't mind. We motor back to the shore and spend the rest of the afternoon on a stony beach, eating sandwiches and picking our way across the rocks. I'm struck by the greyness of it all—the rocks and the mist and the water— and the way the only colour I can see comes from the green pines across the inlet, the golden kelp that's washed ashore. Everything smells of drying life and sharp salt. And this, I realise, is something I love.

In the months after, sensation and my longing for it come to dominate my thoughts, a transformation more aesthetic than intellectual. My hair curls and my period comes. I begin swimming regularly and want always to be in the sea, though this longing is coupled with fear. In pools, I hold my breath and plunge my body to the bottom, feeling the weight of the water as I suspend myself in the deep. I lie in my bed often, imagining I am immersed in salt water, a pattern of shifting light dancing on my bedroom ceiling. I cannot entirely account for it, and perhaps it is a childish wish: I want, if such a thing is possible, to dwell entirely in a world dim-lit, filtered by a haze of plankton. I want the bottom of a shallow sea. I am drawn by colour—by the blue-green of water and olivine light of kelp—more than anything. I tell my friends and family I want to become a marine biologist. But what I really want is to be from the sea. For seaweed to be familiar, not some distant, othered thing.

Even as a child, I know that how I imagine things matters.

At eighteen, I move to the opposite coast—a place equally as grey, where the Atlantic heaves great coils of sugar kelp onto the stones, and the sea makes a shimmering sound as the waves rush out.

I swim whenever I can—bumming rides to Crystal Crescent beach from friends with cars in exchange for discounted lattes at the cafe where I work. We light cigarettes from the coil inside the car and play CDs from high school a little too loud. On the beach, I swim as far as the cold allows me, shivering with fear as I look down and see only dark. The sea, I know then, is bigger than me—unfathomable. The seaweeds on the shore are longer than my whole, still-girlish body.

I turn inward from the world and spend the years after in books. I am not on track to become a biologist; instead I am thinking of philosophy, then art, then beauty. But I'm wishing I was outside, still wanting to feel the sea. I get a degree, then a masters, then a PhD. In the end, most of my work takes place on land—writing about natural beauty and landscape history, cataloguing plants I see and the etymologies of their names. Researching where plants come from and how they entwine with us. Only rarely do I get to be in water, but when I do, I still find myself recoiling from the weeds that brush my legs.

How can I love something I remain afraid of?

I decide I need to think about seaweeds objectively—hold them out in front of me like ideas to think with. To see new facets of their beauty and power.

Rusty, a professor I meet during my doctorate, passes me a book—her own book—about the histories of women and plants. I'm taking a course called Women and Nature, and each week we move forward a century in history and literature. I read about women who spent their days cataloguing algae in the eighteenth and nineteenth centuries, when it became fashionable for women to botanise. Plants were an ideal pastime, as it was often possible to gather, examine, and document specimens around or near the home—and it was largely encouraged socially, provided the species chosen were deemed "polite." Without showy, sexualised flowers, seaweeds—like other nonflowering plants reproducing by spores—were considered particularly suitable for women to study. Algae, and seaweeds especially, therefore became something of a fashion.

Despite the tendency within botanical societies to sideline women's scientific contributions, seaweeds were an area in which women saw unusual success. Over the course of a few weeks I learn of a group Rusty calls the seaweed sorority: a diffuse network of women who pioneered the study of algae in the early nineteenth century. There is Amelia Griffiths, who sent samples to male botanists who prized her abilities for identifying new species. At least two species of algae are named for her. Anna Atkins was raised amidst the scientific milieu of the time and illustrated her father's translation of Lamarck's *Genera of Shells* before turning to photography. Her 1840s cyanotypes of seaweed were published as an illustrated guide—considered the first book illustrated with photographic images, not just by a woman, but by anyone—merging art and science in a historic record of seaweeds on the Kent shore. Margaret Gatty, who wrote for children and adults alike, found in the act of botany a moral vocation. Isabella Gifford, the author of *The Marine Botanist*, never married and instead devoted herself to her scientific work. She found in nature an expression of the divine, and her writings as a result centre seaweeds as essential to all creation, necessary not simply for their beauty but as plants upon which other ocean creatures and humans rely. Following her death, she was herself described by the *Journal of Botany* as part of an essential circle: the "last link of the chain of lady phycologists" of the era.

Wanting to know the women better, I botanise online, learning about seaweeds through digital archives of their work. I click through a collection of Atkins's cyanotypes. These are seaweeds collected nearly two centuries ago, but still their images are so sharp. Like shells or fossils set into paper. Stark imprints of white against China-blue backdrops, they remind me of the foam that gathers where the ocean ends. In each, the seaweeds are carefully arranged, fronds dancing on the page as though they were standing in water.

I scroll the yellowed, digitised pages of *British Sea-Weeds*, the two-volume 1872 opus by Margaret Gatty. She famously roved the shoreline in shorter-than-usual petticoats to avoid dampening them in the sea. She advocated that any woman thinking of following in her footsteps on the "shore-hunt" ought to make use of thick gloves and sturdy boy's shooting boots made waterproof with neat's-foot oil, the way fishermen would. Sticks, she wrote, were ideal appendages for the woman seaweed hunter, being useful both "in rock-clambering and for drawing floating sea-weeds from the water." But even for Gatty, women collectors could access only those parts of nature that polite society deemed acceptable: seaweeds that required one to wade in the shallows or to swim, for example, remained the territory of men. Women were hampered by the draperies of Victorian fashion but had to make do: "Never mind," Gatty writes repeatedly in the text, as she encourages prospective botanisers to familiarise themselves with the tides and local geography. All the better to navigate rock pools, coastal caves, and ebbing tides. Despite its limitations, her seashore is a world of sensuous, vivid language: "The Laminarian zone," the low-water mark where brown seaweed thrives. "Bright bay" and "tufts of jointed threads." In Gatty's pages, there are filaments "like pale brown wool. Stiff, unruly, leathery olive algae."

After the turn of the twentieth century, a new generation of female algologists was on the horizon. Reading about aquaculture, I find article after article about a British woman dubbed the "Mother of the Sea." I read how Japanese fishermen erected a statue to her in 1963. Phycologist Kathleen Mary Drew-Baker had never set foot in Japan, but her studies of seaweed have been credited with saving the nation's nori industry. In the late 1940s, Japan's nori production stalled. Season after season, the farms that normally cultivated plentiful seaweed on sticks thrust into tidal waters came up empty following a series of typhoons and the wreckage of war. But some twenty years earlier in Britain, Drew-Baker had begun experimenting with the

Welsh *Porphyra* alga and was the first to document the life cycle of the species. Having filled an experiment tank with water and *Porphyra*, she tossed in some shells, upon which the alga's spores soon settled. Given time, the shells grew covered in a fine, pink, filmy alga. This species, until then, had been described as *Conchocelis rosea*, but watching her experiment tank closely, Drew-Baker soon realised that this was simply the juvenile phase of *Porphyra*. The seaweed relied on the shells of bivalves to reproduce, something unknown before. Drew-Baker's research, finally published in *Nature* in 1949, solved a vital puzzle needed to revive the Japanese nori industry: Most of the oyster beds that had helped sustain the industry had been decimated by mines, coupled with stormy weather that had destroyed the existing seabed. So Japanese researchers armed with Drew-Baker's findings helped restore what was once a thriving industry.

In a 1958 issue of the *European Journal of Phycology*, I turn up page after page of tributes to Drew-Baker, all attesting to her centrality in the field, to the unresolvable loss of her death. Algae were plants with which female botanists were allowed to thrive—from the earliest days of the botanical boom to the mid-twentieth century. But still, phycology remains a niche science. Reading all this, I wonder if the women who studied seaweeds felt something of kinship for their central—but visibly marginal—role in our world. Like seaweeds, how much of their lives went unnoticed.

How can a world unseen beneath the waves become familiar to us?

While Margaret Gatty bemoaned the difficulty of reaching species in deeper waters and on dangerous outcrops, contemporary scientists have likewise been limited by their abilities to observe, collect, and map seaweeds in place. Mapping a species has long required, for example, that researchers work in submerged and sometimes dangerous conditions. Recent years have seen scientists turn to remote sensing to record seaweed communities that remain submerged: recording their numbers through aerial and satellite imagery, working from colour and shadow to know what exists undersea.

More often, we come to know pelagic worlds when they thrust themselves into our own: when seaweeds arrive on the shore or turn up in places we don't expect or want them to.

In Ruth Ozeki's mesmerising 2013 novel *A Tale for the Time Being*, the protagonist, also called Ruth, discovers a Hello Kitty lunch box filled with a Japanese teen girl's belongings, all wrapped in a Ziploc bag. They've washed ashore on the coast of British Columbia, carried across the

Pacific following the Japanese tsunami. The package glints out at her like a jellyfish from beneath a tangle of bull kelp, a talisman of past disaster and a literal embodiment of the migrations the ocean makes possible.

Ozeki's plot was a reflection of reality. In 2012, fifteen months after the Tōhoku earthquake brought the sea to shore, a dock from Japan's Aomori Prefecture washed up on Agate Beach in Oregon. Its arrival had, for some months, been expected: the National Ocean and Atmospheric Administration had been working to predict and map debris flows from the tsunami, calculating timings and risk and potential trajectories. The sixty-six-foot long concrete and steel dock, according to the EPA's blog, was "covered with organisms not native to North America, including sea stars, barnacles, mussels, amphipods, and algae."

In the weeks after the dock's arrival in Oregon, news articles listed the names of species like enemy troops landing for war. Two oceans and a decade away, I click through articles from PBS, NPR, *The Guardian*, and a website called Oregon Live. I want to know how this story was told. How these nonnative organisms—forced by nature to cross an ocean before being scraped from the dock's surface, sampled, burned, and buried—would be characterised. The dock had been "cut loose," one article tells me, then lists the ways other examples of beached debris have been destroyed: "explosives, napalm, and a torpedo." The dock and all that it carried, I learn, were staging an invasion. And while experts didn't think it was likely to be radioactive, it was, by all accounts, a dangerous piece of flotsam.

I read lists of the species recorded as having made the five-thousand-mile journey. There are brown and red algae, sea lettuce, and other seaweeds. On a university website, I zoom in on a collaged image of the species. The larger animals are named and pictured, but the smaller creatures merely gestured towards: "4+ species of barnacle, 11 species of mollusc, 3+ species of amphipod." I read about the Japanese shore crab—which "reproduces many times a year, and can quickly outnumber and displace native crabs"—and the Northern Pacific seastar, with its "voracious appetite," which could "devastate native species on which it would prey." And amongst them all, I notice a familiar name: wakame kelp.

Culinarily, *Undaria pinnatifida* is prized for its sweetness and texture. Being quite tender, it is well-suited to salads and soups, where it floats, diaphanous, unlike other thicker, squidgier kelps. Amongst invasion biologists, however, the species is classed as being one of the world's worst invasive species, and in Europe, "the third most invasive seaweed." Indigenous to the coasts of East Asia, wakame thrives in the fringes of the sublittoral zone near the shore: from low tide up to eighteen metres in depth, in shallow waters, estuaries, and—as if to underscore the degree to which our fates are bound—on anthropogenic structures like docks.

And not simply due to the anomalies of floating docks, but thanks largely to the ship hulls and ballast waters of our cargo industries, wakame is now a species with a "global nonnative range." Read that again: it is everywhere, but it is still out of place.

Wakame now grows steadily along the coasts of Britain and Europe, Australasia, and the Americas. And while eradication programmes have held little success, some are turning to other possibilities, like farming and harvesting the kelp for commercial uses.

Most winter afternoons, I cook rice cake soup flecked with green strips of invasive wakame. I crumble it into instant noodles and stir fries, offering my body a vegetarian source of iodine and B vitamins. Reading the packet, I learn that the seaweed I buy is hand-harvested off the Spanish and Portuguese coasts, by a company based in Galicia. Their Instagram grid shows underwater photos of free divers clutching nets heaving with algae, between recipe inspo and product placements. There is no mention of wakame as invasive; photos of it are simply hashtagged with words like "conservation" and "ecology." Wakame is a "superfood."

And this is where my hope to know seaweeds on their own terms—as something beyond our uses and classifications of it—dissolves. Because seaweeds remain bound to us and our human stories. Because our own movements around this globe cannot easily be undone. As we drive our desires across the world, the seaweeds are our passengers.

So what worlds do seaweeds make possible?

I stay up late into the night scrolling through thirty-second videos on my phone, though I rarely linger long enough to watch them through. I swipe through recipe demos, travel clips, and parenting advice. Eventually, I land on a video of a kelp forest. It is short—just fifteen seconds long—but it is enough to make me pause.

We swim—I say "we," for the viewers are given the first-person perspective in this video—through a body of water perhaps fifteen metres deep. The water is deep blue below, the colour of a cloud above. Light filters down in bright bands from the surface, and we pan smoothly across a mass of waving kelp. Copper brown and green, the fronds stand upright, suspended as though from above, rather than emerging from the rocky bed below. A large fish, I am not sure what kind, weaves through the forest against a sonic background of jazzy, lo-fi beats. I take my finger off the screen and let the video play, repeat, the electronic piano looping, the swim through an otherworld without end. It is the calmest I've felt in weeks.

I may never be closer to a kelp forest. Kelp forests cover nearly a quarter of the world's coastlines, where they help prevent coastal erosion and sequester enormous amounts of the carbon we are so readily releasing into the atmosphere. But few, save divers and those who make their livings on the coast, spend any time up close with them. Like distant melting glaciers, or viruses we carry but cannot see, it can be hard to make sense of how seaweeds we rarely witness are integral to life on Earth.

But our ways of thinking about seaweeds have much to do with the fate of kelp forests. Whether we write them off as simply weeds, as other. Seaweeds rely on us, too, for the stories we tell about them.

Off the coast of South Africa, in the patch of ocean recently made famous by the documentary *My Octopus Teacher*, campaigners are now working to cultivate an identity for a wild kelp forest in the hopes of conserving it. The Great African Seaforest, so-named by the network of storytellers, filmmakers, and scientists at the Sea Change Project, is a crucially biodiverse ecosystem.

Giant kelp, *Macrocystis pyrifera*, thrives in water between ten and fifteen degrees Celsius (fifty and sixty degrees Fahrenheit), and the oceans can no longer be relied on to stay in that range. As we warm the world, kelp forests are disappearing: in Australia and Tasmania, for example, just 5 percent of the once-vast forest remains.

And we now know that seaweeds hold the records of such transformations fast in their bodies: at the Ocean Memory Lab in California, century-old seaweed samples have been used to extract data on oceanic conditions of the past. Herbarium specimens collected by nineteenth-century algologists and hobbyists now serve as a record for marine science, often predating our contemporary records. These seaweeds store information in their tissues that enables scientists to extend the historical data record for things like upwelling, where nutrients are thrust from the depths to the surface, and pollution. Scientists are able to chart the future of ocean health through these benchmarks from the past.

And beyond these pasts and threatened presents, algae has come to occupy an imagined future for our world. We are dreaming of seaweeds beyond the sea.

Some fourteen thousand years ago, several species of seaweed made their way into the hearths of humans in the southern regions of Chile. 1700 years ago, Zuo Si wrote of tsu-tsai (purple vegetable, *Porphyra* sp.) grown—and used—in abundance. Western knowledge of seaweed cultivation dates back to the seventeenth century, when colonial powers confronted East and Southeast Asian aquaculture: arrays of rocks on which laver could grow, tree branches and bamboo sunk into the shallows for seaweeds to latch on to. But how to capture and control the growth of seaweeds remained unclear until knowledge of its spore patterns—documented by Drew-Baker—became widespread. Only then could cultivation of seaweeds take on an industrial scale—a shift that took place in the 1950s across Asia, but only recently in the West. Now, kelp and other algae are becoming cogs in an industrially farmed tomorrow. North American and European agriculture are poised to turn towards aquaculture—with seaweeds described by journalists as the "food and fuel of the future."

Where I once browsed seaweeds in historic botany books, I now click through articles about seaweeds in the business and innovation sections of the news. I bring up videos where drones fly over flat black seas crisscrossed with ropes. In this future-present, algae is grown from suspended ropes, in tanks, and from enormous cultivation rigs laid upon the seabed. Seaweeds are used to sequester carbon on large scales, acting as mechanisms in a carbon-credit system. They serve as fodder for potential biofuels and emissions-reducing feed for livestock. They have become bioplastics, and proteins from algae have been genetically manipulated into more drought-tolerant tobacco crops. In Singapore, an entrepreneur builds a vertical algae farm, where seaweed grows upwards in tanks, far from the sea. Western seaweed farmers are called pioneers. Investors wear white shirts and speak about profitability. A United Nations report calls seaweed farming a "scalable climate change" solution. The language around seaweed farming today evokes sustainability—underscoring how deeply our thinking about it is bound up with the future—but in every case I come across, these plants are mobilised in capitalist terms: *Seaweed is a good investment. Seaweed will be as big as salmon farming. It will be bigger than potatoes.* Seaweed will solve so many of our problems.

But while many of these farms seem little different from land-bound monocultures, there are those—enterprising fishermen seeking livelihoods beyond fish—who grow their seaweeds in polycultures. Who think of their farms as buffers against storm surges and as new habitats for aquatic life. Smaller in scale, but just as optimistic in their dreams.

Standing on the shore in Margate, battered by wind, it is hard to imagine all this could come from the kelp tangled around my boots. This is one of Britain's richest regions for seaweeds—and much of the world's recent history has touched here, too. Wireweed from the Americas now grows, rafting and drifting in clusters that disperse other creatures along these shores. It has been described as perhaps the most successful invasive in the United Kingdom. And though efforts to eradicate the species have been largely unsuccessful, and there remains a lack of obvious commercial use for it in Europe, researchers look East for ideas: It is eaten in Korea, they write. It is used in aquaculture in China.

Seaweeds may transgress human borders, but they are also bound up with how we imagine the future. They are repositories of our greatest fears and grandest ambitions:

climate change and ecological collapse, carbon capture and cultivation. Being weeds, they unpick scientific paradigms, politics, and nationalisms. All the things that ask for circumstances, species, and people to stay in place.

Rain falls in fat drops upon the sea, and seabirds swoop towards the tide-exposed reef. I've counted eight seaweeds on the sand today, and I'm not yet finished. The dog shakes sand from his fur, sniffs at an open oyster shell. I walk the beach, dodging waves, knowing that seaweeds teach us to soften the hard borders of our human worlds.

6.

Words for Tea

IN MY CHILDHOOD, "TEA" MEANT TWO DIFFER-
ent things: milky, toffee-hued warmth drunk from a white
porcelain mug with one set of grandparents; and golden,
floral heat doled out into tiny cups during dim sum with
the other. For us, as for many, tea was comfort, refresh-
ment. It was through drinking tea that I learned to love bitterness. The astringent liquor at the bottom of my teacup,
unsweetened, coating the back of my throat.

At my nan's house, we each had a cup that was ours.
Mine, a yellow-striped mug with a finger-width handle.
It was here that I learned about colour: Nan taught me to
paint, but also taught me to pour milk into cups of tea, how
much depending on whose cup it was. I learned how I liked
mine, biscuit-hued, a streak of pale milk unstirred. Each
afternoon, I carried the full cups on a little enamel tray

printed with the image of Princess Diana, with a little plate of biscuits sitting off to the side. There were Digestives and Cadbury Fingers somehow scrounged up in suburban Canada. Welsh cakes on the days Nan made them. Tea was an act of care, a way of saying welcome. A portal to the home my grandparents had left in South Wales. Tea was the interlude in conversations where a person didn't quite know what to say.

On my mother's side of the family, tea was drunk amidst noise: loud lunchtime conversation, in clinking cups that I learned how to pour for my Taiwanese elders when I was still a small child. I learned never to let the cups run dry, learned to flip the lid of the teapot when I needed more hot water. We drank jasmine tea mostly, amber-tinted and bittersweet, a perfect foil for the salt of soy. Taro rolls and luobogao left slicks of oil on my plate, but tea washed my mouth clean. Steam rose from the table and from the tiny cup I clutched in my hands.

These two teas were not the same thing, at least not outwardly. And I can't imagine a scene in which my grandparents might drink one another's versions of the same drink. The idea strikes me now, decades after their deaths, as bizarre. I never thought of these teas as the product of the same plant, *Camellia sinensis*. And never considered the many centuries of that plant's movement across our world—and how its twin cultural histories were written in my own body.

With tiny white flowers and toothed leather-green leaves tapered to a point, the tea plant grows as a shrub or a tree in the wild from the Himalayan foothills to the southwest of China. Over lifetimes of up to thousands of years, the tea tree—not to be confused with the Australian species *Melaleuca alternifolia*, from which we get tea tree oil—can grow up to fifteen or twenty metres. The tree is thought to have originated, along with rice, citrus, and a wealth of other crops, in the Eastern Himalayan corridor, through which human migration into Asia once passed. It is, therefore, a plant inextricably tied to movement.

Tea cultures go back as far as these migrations. Looking at the Chinese word for "tea," 茶 (chá), I see leaves growing atop a mountain farm. But the character is more complex than that: tea is built from radical 140 for "grass" (艹), radical number 9 for "people" (人). Cultivated in Asia as a shrub for its young leaf buds, the cultures around the plant's domestication and use have had some five thousand years to develop. As the character reminds us, tea is a plant understood by its entwinement with people.

In European records, tea has been documented only over the past five hundred years. In 1753 the Swedish botanist Linnaeus—famous for formalising plant nomenclature in the West—classified the plant, though he'd never seen it in the field. Working from samples sent to him by another collector, he called the plant *Thea sinensis* (Chinese tea), later going on to divide this classification into *Thea bohea* (black tea) and *Thea viridis* (green tea). But this distinction was soon proven erroneous, as these two are one and the same plant, now called *Camellia sinensis*.

It is a modest species amongst the showier camellias. Unlike the thousands of hybridised ornamental camellias that line garden beds, bursting with bright, many-petalled flowers, the tea plant is mostly green and leafy, dotted sparsely with modest blooms. Despite this difference, the ornamental camellias share a long history of confusion with the tea plant: when brought to Europe from the Philippines and China by botanists in the eighteenth century, *Camellia japonica* was originally classified as *Thea sinensis*. Further confusion between the tea plant and other camellias abounded, in part because drinkable tea can be produced from the leaves of some other species in the genus.

I labour this point because, as much as Western botanists sought to understand and systematise the plant knowledge they gathered on journeys abroad, their knowledge of useful plants like tea remained patchy well into the nineteenth century, despite its economic import. This lack of knowledge and the need to rectify it would influence Britain's relationship with tea-producing regions in profound—and not unproblematic—ways.

In the seventeenth and eighteenth centuries, plants and their products crossed the globe in all directions—with new-world plants brought to Europe just as old-world plants were carried across the globe by colonists seeking to reproduce their familiar floras elsewhere. Tea, like many introduced goods, enjoyed a rapid rise in popularity in Britain after its introduction in the 1650s. But the gulf between the tea plant and processed tea remained wide; without knowledge of how best to actually process the leaves into a palatable drink, British importers remained desperately reliant on trade with China, which strictly controlled the production and export of tea.

Initially British sales of tea imported from China were taxed enormously and thus, along with sugar, fuelled funds back into the workings of empire, particularly to the Royal Navy and British East India Company. But despite the cost, a century after its introduction, once duties were repealed and prices dropped, it had become even more popular than beer. It was served at breakfast and in the afternoons and, despite its still relatively high price, was accessible for both the aristocratic and everyday person.

As tea enjoyed its rise in European society, tobacco and opium poppies likewise found popular use. In China, where the two were used in tandem, demand for opium traded by the British East India Company facilitated British access to tea, for which the Chinese would only accept silver. Britain wasn't especially rich with silver, so grew its wealth in part through trading opium grown in British colonies in India. Britain was reliant upon this trade, but after a Chinese imperial edict banning the opium trade in 1753, it became largely illicit, with the drug transported by frigate to smugglers in China. By 1773, Britain had become China's leading supplier of opium. Over decades, amidst China's displeasure at the trade, tensions rose. By 1839—just when professor of the Royal Medico-Botanical Society George Sigmond declared Britain's "national importance" to be "intimately connected with [tea]"—Britain was embroiled in the first Opium War.

This is a tangled history, most of which I cannot tell here. Entire books are needed for that task. But in the story of tea, there are details I cannot overlook.

By the end of the war, though Britain had gained territory ripe for trade in Hong Kong, foreign travel into China aside from treaty ports like Shanghai remained tightly restricted. Stemming the reliance on Chinese trade, the East India Company hoped instead that tea could be produced in colonised land in Assam—largely through indentured labour. Acquiring plants would be simple enough; plant collectors had for some decades secured seeds of moderate quality, which they'd planted in India with very modest success. But high-quality seeds and the actual skills needed to transform them into tea as we know it were things the British lacked.

In 1848, the British East India Company sent Scottish botanist Robert Fortune to China. He'd been recently engaged as curator of the Chelsea Physic Garden, and his previous travels in China had caught the company's attention. Tasked with securing both an adequate supply of quality tea plants as well as the knowledge of how exactly they needed to be processed, and ignoring Chinese imperial bans on foreign incursions into the country, Fortune journeyed inland through Zhejiang and Anhui.

In Fortune's record of the period, *A Journey to the Tea Countries of China*, he writes of an incident prior to his arrival, in which local boatmen had been punished for taking foreigners into the interior of the country. So, on the advice of his servants, in order to reach Hwuy-chow (Huizhou)—"a sealed country to Europeans"—Fortune donned a disguise. "My servants now procured me a Chinese dress, and had the tail which I had worn in former years nicely dressed by the barber . . . To put on the dress was an easy matter, but I had also to get my head shaved . . . I then dressed myself in the costume of the country, and the result was pronounced by my servants and boatmen to be very satisfactory." Dressed and coiffed to pass as Chinese, as though no one would notice the difference, Fortune journeyed farther into China than many Europeans had before, observing the methods for cultivating, picking, drying, and processing tea leaves on his way. At the end of his journey, he hired a number of Chinese specialists to travel to Assam and pass on their skilled trade.

Of course, there had been other options, Fortune admits. He could have hired Chinese agents to travel on his behalf, but he did not trust they would truly make the journey or that the plants and seeds they returned with would be genuine. "No dependence can be placed upon the veracity of the Chinese," he writes. Instead, he undertook the journey himself—describing the voyage as one of "penetration." I do not set out to read Fortune unfairly—he explicitly admits to concerns that the portraits he paints of China are themselves uncharitable. But I feel uneasy about how his efforts are positioned today.

European botany in this period is rich with plant hunters labelled swashbucklers, adventurers, and frontiersmen, often obscuring the local networks of experts, guides, and labourers who helped them secure the plants they then "introduced" to the West. Little in Fortune's story should surprise me. His tale has such a potent hold in popular histories of tea that I find it difficult to overlook. Even in our contemporary moment, Fortune's journeys have been couched as adventurous; in one popular history by Sarah Rose, Fortune is framed as a spy or even a thief. Elsewhere, he is described as a smuggler and a hero.

Alistair Watt, in a biography of Fortune, implores readers not to interpret Fortune's plant transfers within the framework of our present-day thinking about intellectual property or biopiracy—with the skill needed to produce tea regarded as proprietary knowledge—but to view his journeys as part of a period when plants moved in all directions around our world, both from and to imperial powers.

And indeed, as I've mentioned, plant exchange did go both ways in the making of empire. But I cannot read this history without acknowledging that power was mobilised in devastating ways—that the tea trade was tied to the need for sugar, and therefore to the transatlantic slave trade that sustained sugar production in the Caribbean; that Britain built its tea plantations on indentured labour; that efforts to secure what was ultimately unequal trade with China relied predominantly on the peddling of opium.

Thief, spy, adventurer: these framings all fall flat. I cannot bring myself to romanticise Fortune as a swashbuckler or see his actions as innocuous. For we know from even the very recent past—from the toppling of statues of slave traders to the restitution of looted artefacts—that reimagining and reassessing histories of empire are essential acts of decolonising our cultural narratives. Though Chinese tea production simply shifted towards Asian markets and green tea, and away from the British demand for black tea, I cannot forget the words of historian Lucile Brockway: these were circumstances, she wrote, in which "a corps of trained botanists [were] supported by the state and ready to cooperate with the government in removing from a weaker nation a desirable plant for development on British soil, under British control."

I am trained as a historian, but the more I read of Fortune, the more I take this history personally. Sometimes I feel silly about that, caught between a mistaken idea of objectivity and the subjectivity of my own skin. I am mixed race—British, Taiwanese, with my grandparents born in China—yet I have never passed as wholly one or the other. So every time I read about Fortune, every time I find a new framing or defence of his work, I come back to the notion that one day, before setting out, he sewed a queue into his hair and disguised himself in Mandarin dress. As if Chineseness was merely a costume that could be donned.

Tea plants and the drinks we make from them carry so many meanings. The daily, domestic rituals through which I have known tea, in its Chinese, Taiwanese, and British guises. And of course tea is a drink prized across cultures and traditions, not solely my own. Tea is explicitly political: thinking of U.S. history, tea has signified rebellion—and, in present-day iterations of the Tea Party, regressive and populist conservatism. In sixteenth-century Japan, tea ceremonies were put to military and political ends; in 1920s Iran, the popularisation of tea instead of coffee has been credited with dampening political dissent. Tea, the second most popular drink in the world after water, is a way to gather together, a means for marking rites of passage, a stimulant not just of bodily life but of social connection.

Tea, today, remains political: It is primarily grown in areas that are likewise biodiversity hotspots, where monocultures for the plant sit at odds with sustaining local ecologies. As swathes of forest are cleared for tea plantations to meet global demand, other species of the *Camellia* genus face habitat loss and endangerment. The perpetuation of precarious labour practices on tea plantations—from poor pay to unsafe housing conditions and a range of human rights abuses—reminds us that the horrors associated with plantations of the past are not, in fact, behind us.

There's a famous saying that what we call tea in a language depends entirely on the workings of trade during the period of empire: "'Tea' if by sea, 'cha' if by land." If your culture first received tea via trade routes by sea from Fujian in the south of China, your language likely calls it something like the Min Nan (Hokkien) word "te": thé, Tee, tea. If trade over land brought you tea, you likely call it something like the standard Mandarin 茶 (chá): chai, shay, cha. The very notion of movement, of trade and empire, is written into this plant and how we describe it. That one of the most comprehensive recent histories of tea is written not by a historian or botanist but by a linguist—George L. van Driem—is telling.

So how might I begin to think about tea, knowing that the workings of empire are not wholly in the past and cannot entirely be undone? Knowledges and histories shift depending on who's doing the storytelling.

I've begun relearning Mandarin as an adult, making up for the Saturday Chinese school classes I hated as a child. Each week, I meet with my tutor, Mei, online, and she takes me through words I've heard my entire life but never really understood. Sometimes she laughs at the strange gaps in my language, the way I know phrases that now seem old-fashioned because the only person I've ever spoken Mandarin to is my mother, who for the past four decades has lived her life almost entirely in English.

Early in our lessons, Mei asked me to read a dialogue about buying boba milk tea. She played the shopkeeper, I played the customer. When it came time to translate it, she seemed surprised at my fluency in this one exchange: I knew every word for ordering tea, a rare feat in our weekly conversation practice. I confessed that it was one of the first things I forced myself to learn by heart: as if knowing how to order zhēnzhū nǎichá, less ice, half sugar, was a marker of my own belonging in my mother's culture.

Of course, belonging isn't so simple. And thinking it could be may betray my *overseasness*, my place as an outsider looking in. But a kind of strictness and longing to make tea mine is something I've been unable to shake. So I practice ordering: Yībēi níngméng lùchá, shǎo bīng. Liǎng bēi wūlóng chá, rè de.

The city I grew up in doesn't have a Chinatown, though these days the strip malls bustle with hotpot restaurants and boba shops. When I was growing up, we needed to drive two hours to Toronto for such things. We'd park at the multistorey carpark at Dundas and Spadina, climb the concrete steps, and emerge into an alley scented with five-spice and traffic. We'd descend to the basement of Champion House to eat Peking duck, and then Mom would hold my hand as we walked along the block to Ten Ren Tea shop. Without fail, though we visited it every time, she reminded me Ten Ren was a famous Taiwanese brand. I'd nod my head and fill paper cups with tea samples, while she'd stand for what felt like hours chatting with the salesperson, choosing teas that she barely even drank when we got home. I think, looking back, that it made her feel closer to home just to have them around.

In adulthood, I left Canada and moved to Britain. I moved to Germany. Back to Canada, back to the U.K., to Taiwan, and back to Germany again. The more I moved countries and homes myself, the more my mother's tea shopping began to make sense to me. Tea shopping was a way of gathering familiar things close, if only just to hold them. When I last moved back to the U.K., I couldn't find the loose-leaf jasmine tea I like, and it bothered me, irrationally. I skulked in Chinese supermarket aisles, picking up every box of tea to decide if it would suffice, but it never did. Everything seemed to come in bags. Bags! I called my friends and moaned about it. Even though every afternoon, after lunch, my husband and I made cups of milky Yorkshire Tea from tea bags. But jasmine tea felt unnatural to me in this format. Why was I so picky about that one thing, and only in that one context? I suppose I had a sense of how it should be, a fixation on authenticity. I can only say that tea somehow plays on sentiments I cannot fully express, on my sense of routine and ritual. There is a right way to do it.

I think back to the words I use for tea—both words, "tea" and 茶 ("chá")—and am struck by my inability to choose. I cannot think of tea without acknowledging the legacies of my own cultures and their empires. By the way I hold the movements of this plant in my bones.

7.

Dispersals

IT IS HARD TO HEAR HIM SPEAK BENEATH THE roar of lorries on Orient Way. Every few seconds, a petrol-scented tailwind gusts along the roadside, and all the branches shudder. Twelve of us are clustered together on this rewilded footpath next to the park, waiting for guidance on our volunteer conservation session. We are meant to be planting trees, little whips we've carried out in buckets and wheelbarrows, but our leader has stopped to tell us about weeds instead.

"Here is the difference." Jonny reaches his gloved hand towards a leaf the size of his head. "This one is okay to touch. That's the native plant. See how its leaves are more rounded?" He points towards a larger specimen, its leaves jutting out into sharp, toothy points. A line of neon spray paint has been daubed across it. "This one . . . just never, ever touch it." He goes on to describe the phytochemical burns that can be caused by the plant's sap, burns that can persist for many years after contact with it. A young man in my group winces, then glances at the leaves again as if to cement them in memory.

Once Jonny shows us the difference between native and giant hogweed, I'm surprised to realise just how much of the latter grows along the footpath. The spray paint, I learn, is to help the plants stand out when the council comes to destroy it with herbicide. No one seems sure when that'll be. One of the other volunteers, a pensioner in a blue raincoat who attends every session, tells me there is a whole field of giant hogweed growing at a brownfield site nearby. All the hogweed that has seeded along this path, he says, can be attributed to that abandoned plot.

Native originally to Central Asia, giant hogweed has a reputation in Europe and North America as amongst the worst alien invasive species, a weed so vigorous and dangerous that it has been called "the most dangerous plant in Britain." But like nearly all foreign species now considered problematic, giant hogweed was brought to Western Europe as an ornamental, prized through the nineteenth century for its large, showy umbels of white flowers. Beyond the space of the garden, it is a species that thrives on disturbed and neglected ground: riverbanks, railway sidings, abandoned plots. Our local park had once been a Victorian dump, falling between a swathe of neglected plots from Walthamstow to the Olympic Park in Stratford, land that had only recently been seen as "useful" again. Land on which the giant hogweed, we learned, had long since found a home.

On the first page of one of my favourite books about plants, Richard Mabey describes weeds as those plants that "obstruct our plans, or our tidy maps of the world." This phrasing captures a lot: notice the "our," which appears in both clauses, or the word "obstruct," which tells us how we might judge these plants. The last bit—"tidy maps of the world"—has always stood out to me. Because it is on maps that we draw our borders, and it is borders that most plants do not readily recognise. The giant hogweed had jumped the borders of the nearby wasteland and was crowding into the growth along an increasingly busy footpath. A few specimens had made their way over to Hackney Marshes, where over the summer locals dipped along the banks of the River Lea. Dispersed by wind and water, the seeds had made their way from a site of neglect and disuse into territory that—in the wake of Olympic investment—had only recently begun to be swallowed up by property investors.

Admittedly, I've never been that worried by the idea of weeds, perhaps owing to a childhood in a Canadian suburb where herbicide was habitually applied to lawns. At certain times of year, little poison signs on wire wickets would dot the entire neighbourhood, letting us know whose yards had recently been sprayed. The only weeds seemed to be occasional clusters of dandelions and patches of clover that tried futilely to colonise the perfectly green Kentucky bluegrass. Alfred Crosby, analysing the ways plants moved from Britain across the world, declared that "the sun never sets on the empire of the dandelion," but to me, then, they were simply innocuous flowers, trying their best to thrive where they weren't welcomed. It seemed senseless to me that an entire suburb would wield such heavy-handed warfare on a few stray plants. When I was fifteen, I read *Silent Spring* and decided to drop anti-biocide leaflets to all my neighbours, resulting in a lukewarm response from locals and some embarrassment on the part of my family. So you might say an interlude of teenage rebellion too easily dismissed enamoured me of the plants we call weeds.

But the giant hogweed indeed poses a kind of danger. In the weeks after that conservation session, I find myself telling multiple park visitors who've strayed into the shrubbery—one wearing only his swim trunks—that they really do want to avoid touching the plant they are about to touch. I find myself describing photosensitive burns to strangers, keeping a mental inventory of just how many times I see the plant dot this patch of East London. So why do I still feel uneasy about the plants so often derided as problems?

Later in the introduction to *Weeds*, Mabey offers another framing: a weed is simply "a plant in the wrong place." This is a common phrasing and one that calls to mind the tidy definition of "dirt" offered by anthropologist

Mary Douglas as "matter out of place." In her 1966 book *Purity and Danger*, Douglas argues that societies with a ritual of hygiene—that is, those who have a notion of what it means for something to be dirty—are engaging in an effort to organise the environment. It is a creative act, done to create unity and meaning in our experience of the world. Douglas begins by speaking from an anthropological perspective; she contrasts European societal norms with those of other societies in ethnographic terms like "primitive" and "native." But it becomes clear that the notions of purity and danger underpin all our acts and societal beliefs. Contemporary notions of cleanliness are informed by a knowledge of pathogens—bacteria, viruses, knowledge we've had for little more than a century and a half through the work of scientists like Louis Pasteur. Before that, however, we clearly had a notion of what was clean and what was dirty. Through religion and social institutions, we had a system for ordering the world, a symbolic order by which we understood what belonged where. So when we label a plant a "weed"—or to use the terms more often deployed in ecology and conservation, "invasive" or "alien"—we are not just labelling that plant. We are implying a desired order for the world at large.

But this order remains context-specific. Giant hogweed that grows in the Caucasus, where it is considered native, is no more a weed than an oak tree in England. Likewise, the specimens brought by plant collectors into Victorian gardens were, at first, seen as perfectly desirable. Japanese knotweed—a plant now considered so noxious that houses on plots where the species has taken root are often considered unsellable—was once a popular garden plant. The problem occurs when species "jump the garden wall," to borrow a phrase from historian Harriet Ritvo. Mabey notes that even native plants like rosebay willowherb, when too persistent in their spread, might likewise be derided as weeds. The need to create order, however arbitrary, is simply a human habit: as Ritvo writes, "It is the existence of some system of classification, rather than its specific content, that is a human constant."

But our categories are liable to transform, just as the baselines of our knowable world have shifted. As the climate changes, researchers now predict that giant hogweed's range will decrease by the middle of our century. This is not to say it will no longer be invasive; rather, needing cold winters, the hogweed will move northward. Its presence is not a given, but in the context of anthropogenic climate change, we are reminded that we cannot remove ourselves from the story of this plant's invasiveness. Weediness implies movement, but plants do not often move very far without our blessing.

In late summer, we leave East London and move into a rented house in Cambridge so I can be closer to work. The landlord's mother pops by to check on the garden. Mostly, I think, she is gauging my willingness to tend it. She takes inventory of the front garden's shrubbery, teeters from a ladder as she trims back the neighbour's wisteria growing pleasantly over our doorway. Once she is finished, she points to a bare patch of low growth amidst the landscaped sections of the garden. She has laid down weed-resistant membrane, which glows black in the September sun.

"There used to be a buddleia here," she remarks. "But the last tenants tore it out." She frowns, her eyes searching mine for a reply.

"Such a pity!" I say, almost automatically, noting silently that the absence of the plant will bring more afternoon sun into the living room. I don't want to tell her that I'm not bothered by the weeds inching their way through the membrane, that in fact I somewhat like the persistent, irregular patch of growth. But I know, too, that in our row of houses, an untended patch would stick out sorely. That not everyone cares for weeds as I do.

It isn't until months later that I decide to take inventory. I slip into the morning shade and begin to count species that have forced their way through the membrane: evergreen bugloss, cheeseweed mallow, wild teasel, and horseweed. Dead-nettles and dock grow somewhere in between, and dandelions, too. The green stands knee-high, reaching for the sun that stripes the front garden in gold each day. I know some neighbours may not appreciate the teasel, though I love the birds it brings. A few brown spiky stalks remain of last year's seed heads, so it will have spread itself around next door's garden, too. I had thought to pop some pots out here—I've started too many tomatoes and they'd appreciate the west-facing light—but now I wonder if I should actually "weed" the patch. Whether I should lay down native wildflower seeds, or find a way to make the patch look tended. I've come to admire this bit of green outside my window. It is the view from my desk, the ragged growth I look upon while I write. What plants, I ask, do I want to think with?

The need for an order by which to understand plants out of place became particularly acute in the nineteenth century. Plant collecting reached its peak in the century, and new species introductions were transforming landscapes across the world. So in 1847, the botanist Hewett Cottrell Watson published his *Cybele Britannica*, a flora in which he clarified the categories through which he believed plants should be arranged. Drawing on the work of Cambridge botanist John Henslow, Watson described plants in Britain as *native*, *denizen*, *colonist*, *alien*, or *incognita* (meaning the plant's status was unknown). Watson—who was also known as a practitioner of phrenology, the racist pseudoscience of predicting human abilities according to their skulls—had been apprenticed in law before opting to pursue science. So three of the terms he proposed—*native, alien,* and *denizen,* the latter a halfway state between the former two—drew from the language of citizenship law.

His text abounds in efforts to create order. "Arrangement," he writes, "is the first effort of science." And so he labels species according to the borders of nations: the British Type, the English Type, the Scottish, the Highland, Germanic, and Atlantic. Wales does not get its own type.

Eight years later, the Swiss botanist Alphonse de Candolle presented his own interpretation, with categories of *cultivated, adventitious, recently naturalised, formerly naturalised,* and *primitive* or *aboriginal* ("Je voudrais trouver des caractères pour distinguer les plantes *cultivées, adventives, récemment naturalisées,* puis *anciennement naturalisées,* et enfin *primitives* ou *aborigènes*"). He distinguished, crucially, between plants cultivated by humans and those that appeared spontaneously—right of passage deemed a given for plants we garden or farm, so long as they stay in place. Watson, responding to these proposals, clarified that all species that occurred without human agency must "unavoidably" be classed as native. So it was that human intervention would be the deciding factor in whether a plant was seen as belonging.

A century later, when in 1958 the British ecologist Charles Elton published *The Ecology of Invasions by Animals and Plants,* this same emphasis on human intervention came to characterise the distinction between whether a plant was invasive or not. Elton was fascinated with what he termed a "breakdown" of Wallace's realms, the long-standing order by which living beings had arrayed themselves around the world. "The real thing," he wrote, "is that we are living in a period of the world's history when the mingling of thousands of kinds of organisms from different parts of the world is setting up terrific dislocations in nature." This candid tone carries through the text. Intended not for a scientific audience but for a more general reader, the book grew out of a series of broadcasts Elton had given for the BBC, where the programme had been titled *Balance and Barrier*. The word "invasion," the BBC thought, was too reminiscent of war.

The impact of Elton's text was modest at first, but interest in the book came to a head in the 1990s, when concerns around biodiversity began to dominate conservation efforts. Invasive species were being increasingly recognised as a driver of biodiversity loss. For example, Article 8(h) of the 1992 UN Convention on Biological Diversity—now ratified by every member nation except the United States— says that contracting parties should as far as possible "prevent the introduction of, control or eradicate those alien species which threaten ecosystems, habitats or species."

From then on, the fledging field of "invasion ecology" would lend its language to conservation efforts large and small: notions of native species as good and alien invaders

as implicitly bad trickled out into wider public conscious-
ness. Even if the reality recognised by ecologists was far
more complex.

But critics, many taking pains to acknowledge the ecological impact of certain species upon biodiversity, soon
raised concerns about the field's terminology. A debate
raged, and continues, as to whether racism and xenophobia
sit at the heart of attempts to classify some species as "native" and others as "alien invasives." The language around
whether a species belongs, critics argued, too often drifts
uncomfortably close to notions of purity. In 2001, tracing
the rise of globalisation and subsequent interest in conserving what was perceived as "local," Banu Subramaniam
described the hyperbolic and alarmist language with
which rightful concern about species was framed in terms
of racial panic. She cites news article titles—"'Alien invasions: they're green, they're mean, and they may be taking
over a park or preserve near you'" for example—noting the
ways the plants themselves are obfuscated by fear-based
language. If the tide of outsiders cannot be stemmed,
the story goes, nature as it was once known will not be
recovered.

These concerns did not emerge from nowhere. In the
decades before Elton wrote his text, racism and fascism
had indeed made appeals to nature to justify movements
for national, racial, or ethnic purity: In Germany, the legacy of a Nazi obsession with romantic ideas of Heimat and

with plant species seen as rightfully German taints notions of national landscape today. An English fascist obsession with the "green and pleasant land" and white indigeneity (while often voting for policies that result in that land's enclosure and devastation) remains at the root of British environmentalism and, indeed, nature writing, still largely uninterrogated.

I do not mean to rehash this debate in arguing that invasion ecology is inherently racist. It is an argument that too often distinctly reifies C. P. Snow's argument that two cultures—the sciences and the humanities—exist divided, with both sides arguing that they've been misunderstood. I do, however, mean to underscore the non-neutrality of the language it employs—and to argue that language matters.

It becomes increasingly difficult to draw lines around human interventions: from species that hitchhike on the bottoms of shoes, tyres, or ship ballasts, to those we've intentionally transported in Wardian cases. What do we make of those whose seeds we have selected over generations, and those we've transformed in laboratory settings?

Finding a baseline before which our interventions in nature are deemed "natural" is difficult—the International Commission on Stratigraphy's Anthropocene Working Group, for example, has worked for more than a decade to define the terms by which we might understand our impact on the planet. But these questions are not new: that even nineteenth-century texts on plant introductions highlight

the anthropogenic forces that shape such plants' movements, I think, forces us to interrogate where and when, exactly, we might locate a version of nature to which we would
like to return. At what point do we decide an intervention
in the natural world is acceptable? And at what point do we
acknowledge that the environmental legacies of the great
acceleration cannot be treated distinctly from the social,
cultural, very human power dynamics that shaped them?
So much biological control, in our world shaped by nations
and treaties, is subject to our shifting geopolitical borders.

In March of 2023, the Botanical Society of Britain and
Ireland published their *Plant Atlas 2020*, a painstaking survey of plants across the archipelago. Strikingly, they found
that introduced species now outnumber native species in
Britain (1,753 nonnative species versus 1,692 native species).
How, then, can we dwell in a zone of imperfection—managing some species while accepting others, *in language that
does the same*—when centuries of global transformation
cannot be, and wouldn't desirably be, undone?

There are, of course, alternatives proposed, particularly
as scientists worry that problematic terminology may cloud
the actual problems presented by some species. "Indigenous" and "non-Indigenous." "Donor regions" and "novel
environments." "Introduced species" and categories like
"Stage 0" or "Stage V" to indicate the degree to which a
species has moved. Some propose to do away with the "immigrant" status of species altogether, opting instead for a

framework built around impact—and most important, damage. Implicit in this idea is a notion that there was once a time when nature was pristine.

When summer arrives, the teasel and dead-nettles still grow out front. Grass begins to encroach upon their territory, and soon the patch is tall and pale brown. The whole neighbourhood is dry and sun-scorched, the leaves of every green plant dusty and muted. I've been tasked with watching over my neighbour Becky's allotment while she travels. Each morning, before the sun is too high, I wander over, taking stock of how her plants are growing. I fill watering cans from the metal cisterns and douse the raised beds. The broad beans are covered in aphids, so these I water from higher up, hoping to knock a few of them off. I notice the salad bed is choked with bindweed. It winds its way around the bed's wooden posts, in between the leaves of lettuce. I'm worried the plot won't thrive if I don't intervene. I text Becky, but she tells me simply that she likes the look of bindweed's flowers, that I needn't worry. After the plot, I walk the dog in the park by the churchyard. Foxtails catch in his white fur, and I know I'll have to remove them later on. On the way back, we practice loose lead walking, him struggling to remain in heel, along the streets around DeFreville Avenue.

It is on one of these walks that I notice the hollyhock.

It grows outside the wall of a redbrick house, taller than the boxwood next to it and taller than me. It is thick and knotted along its stem and has forced its way through the concrete where the low stone wall meets the pavement. Farther along, I see a hollyhock just as persistent has been felled and left prostrate on the ground. A bumblebee still nurses from its blooms, though the leaves are beginning to desiccate in the heat. When I get home, wondering what the difference might be between the hollyhocks and my persistent patch of weeds, I look the flowers up on the Royal Horticultural Society's website. They are "stalwarts of the cottage garden," the website tells me, and though they are not native to Britain they've been growing here since at least the fifteenth century. These are not plants out of place, however much they may press at the borders of these quiet streets. Hollyhocks, however forceful in their growth, belong.

I do not think our orders for the world are fixed. I think of Elton, about how the language of his work was softened to suit the tastes of the day. I think of giant hogweed moving northward, our planet's familiar cycles shifting. Our language shifts, too. It must.

The next day, we take a route down a shaded avenue. At the end, I see a house fronted entirely by pinks and reds and oranges, hollyhocks flaming against the yellow brick. I stop for a while to look at the flowers closely. They have taken over the entire garden and have begun drifting towards the pavement. They've wrapped themselves around a road sign. No one is cutting them back. The hollyhocks brighten the road and my morning. They venture beyond the wall together, reaching for light carried from the western sky.

8.

Bitter Greens

PAST THE DAGENHAM BROOK IN EAST LONDON, at the far end of an industrial estate, is the Longdan Vietnamese supermarket's warehouse. A huge storage area gives way to a tiny shopfront, concrete floored and brightly lit under fluorescent bulbs. The blue gates to the estate sit permanently open, and a forklift remains parked at the warehouse's loading bay. Two or three shopping carts stand always ready for restauranteurs to load up with industrial quantities of rice or fish sauce. Lemongrass and chillies. From the corners of the brickwork outside, whatever the season, a few plucky green weeds grow.

I've become used to ignoring these surroundings when I walk to buy noodles and tofu at the grocer, not because I don't like living in East London—not exactly—but because I find the road too busy and the pavements too narrow for a pandemic. The weeds begin to catch my eye, though.

From one nearby corner, dandelion grows up thick around a pile of perpetual litter. Around the gates and buildings at Longdan, there is field mustard. Green leaves grown dusty in the outflow of car exhaust.

That March, I plant a tray of bok choy seedlings using a packet of seed I found in the refrigerator section of Longdan. I stood in front of the seed packets for ages, knowing how little space I had at home for growing: just three deep window boxes I'd bared of geraniums a few weeks earlier. I decided on a shining silver packet of Shanghai bok choy seeds, knowing that this was something I cooked and ate often. A familiar crop—except while I'd normally find it in the supermarket, airfreighted and chilled, I wanted it to come from my kitchen window.

I start the tiny brown seeds in two plastic takeaway containers, lids propped open to mimic the warmth and air of greenhouses. Ten days later, puckered green leaves emerge from the soil, stretching higher and faster than anything else I've grown before. Within a few weeks, they curl towards the sunlight and begin to resemble miniature bok choys, the size of a fridge magnet. In mid-April, I plant them outside, protected from slugs and snails with a small fence of copper chicken wire my husband crafts using chopsticks and a wire cutter.

In the weeks that follow, I cut their outer leaves, taking care with my scissors so that the tender cores might continue to grow. I use them in soups and curries, letting the plants redouble their efforts while still in the soil. And grow they do as I use them: thick emerald leaves replaced by smaller ones in jade and white. I know that by May it will be too hot for bok choy—brassicas tend to prefer cooler weather—but I leave each head planted to live out its full life cycle, bolting towards the sun.

The weeds I saw growing from the brickwork outside Longdan and those I planted and tended, these were related plants, though they seemed far distant from one another. In the gap between them fell a question: What does this plant teach us about care and attention?

Most plants we eat have been reshaped by human hands: ancestors, Indigenous people, farmers, plant breeders, and scientists. Few plants, however, give our diets quite as much variety as brassicas. Bok choy is a subspecies of *Brassica rapa*, one of the many brassica species we have metamorphosed through cultivation over thousands of years. Rapini, turnip, and Chinese cabbage (also known as napa) are all likewise cultivars or subspecies of *Brassica rapa*, shepherded towards different forms based on our preference for flowers, roots, or leaves.

Taken together, brassicas provide a greater diversity of crops than any other single genus cultivated on Earth. The species *Brassica oleracea*, like *Brassica rapa*, gives us a range of crops we often forget are from the same ancestor: broccoli, cauliflower, Brussels sprouts, kale, cabbage, kohlrabi, amongst others. *Brassica napus* cultivars give us canola oil as well as fodder and forage for livestock.

A "cultivar," or cultivated variety, is a type of plant bred for its desired characteristics. Our desires, human as they are, determine what that plant will be. That we can name so many familiar foods and crops all stemming from one genus of plants is the result of a process of careful—and sometimes incidental—domestication and transformation. Changes that occur in small steps over many years, in this case, centuries or millennia. So a seed selected from a particularly showy inflorescence is eventually, over many generations, shepherded towards broccoli, while an especially tight leaf cone one day gives us cabbage. Cultivars are the product of careful selection, accidental discovery, patience, and long attention.

Undomesticated, the brassicas are scrappy plants, well-suited to dry soil and drought-like conditions. The two I know best—*Brassica rapa* like I bought at Longdan and wild cabbage (*Brassica oleracea*), in its wild form more common by the seashore—are both identifiable by their blue-green leaves and delicate yellow flowers. In the wild, the leaves will be smaller, duller, and thicker than those of the cultivars, but fundamentally, they are not a world away from the plants we eat. The versions we have selected for ourselves simply favour other features: large flower heads, thin leaves, compact heads.

But as with many familiar cultivars, exactly how they came to be cabbages, turnips, broccoli, and kale is uncertain. So during the summer that I grow bok choy from the windowsill, I trace brassicas through time. And I find our stories more entwined—at times more uncertain—than I have ever imagined.

What the records tell us is this: human desire is a powerful thing. It is also ephemeral, lost in the moment it is felt, though its traces remain in the world long after. From a swelled root to a crinkled leaf: in the plants we eat, there are remnants of our search for the medicinal and the palatable, and in their genetic makeup, a record of our movements between places.

Brassica rapa, thought to be originally native to the Fertile Crescent, has been domesticated across Asia for so long its exact movements have become opaque. Understanding its story requires researchers to consider two parallel paths: scholars trace not just genetic and molecular records of brassicas across geographies and time, but corroborate these searches through references to the plants in ancient literature. Plant geneticists cite classical texts, and botanical scholars unearth the linguistic roots of plant names from the pages of old books.

In the case of *Brassica rapa*, genetic studies remain unclear as to whether it was domesticated multiple times in multiple places, or just once—most likely in Central Asia—and then carried along Silk Road trade routes. Its value has crossed cultures and continents: seeds of the species have been documented in Neolithic and Bronze era excavations in Europe, while some of the earliest mentions of the species are said to have been more than three thousand five hundred years ago in the Sanskrit Upanishads. Its subspecies—from turnips to Chinese cabbage—exist in Chinese records going back more than two and a half thousand years, from the *Shī jīng* to the Tang dynasty *Bencao* (materia medica, an atlas of medicinal plants) compiled by Su Jing, dating to 659 CE. It is surmised by the genetic record and corroborated by literary sources that the turnip was most likely the first cultivar to be developed from the species, from a wild relative in an uncertain place. There followed bok choy and eventually, in what is perhaps a happy accident, perhaps an intentional crossing of bok choy with turnip, the Chinese cabbage. Searches through the genome of *Brassica rapa* subspecies present a cultivation history that roughly correlates with that of literature: the genetic record tells us when each variety may likely have emerged, and this maps well onto the records of written history.

Brassica oleracea—the source of broccoli and other

European brassicas—has a relatively shorter history, thought to have been cultivated for over two thousand years. Studies of the plant's history in literature have been more productive than that of *rapa*, in part because of this shorter timeline. This approach presumes that the longer a species has been in one place, the more likely it is that words for it proliferate, while where plants have been introduced from elsewhere, the words for them tend to come already attached. Scholars have thus mined ancient Greek and Latin texts, tracing words thought to be at the root of our contemporary common names for brassicas: βράσκη (braske), καυλός (kaulos), κράμβη (krambe). Brassica, caulis, crambe. It isn't a long distance from these words to those I use today: "kohl" in German, "col" in Spanish. Ancient Greek echoes when I speak the name of the cauliflower.

By tracing the places these words do appear and when, scholars attempt to reconstruct the journey of brassicas between Europe and Asia. But it is not a watertight way of understanding the world: while a Mediterranean home for *Brassica oleracea* has been proposed, so too has a North Atlantic one. The Celts, presumed to have domesticated the brassicas growing on rocky Atlantic coasts, transmitted their histories largely orally, so cannot be ruled out. While the genetic record can help in narrowing the movements of the plant, answers at times escape us.

In tracking descriptions, synonyms, and the seeds of our contemporary words for brassicas, even genetic scholars demonstrate how our knowledge of plants relies on history, stories, and language. As much as the transformations of these crops have been a product of human care, and as much as we seek to qualify their existence through science, efforts to understand and trace the transformations also rely on the things we'd conventionally deem "culture." These twin paths—the scientific and the literary—seek to inscribe a boundary between the wild forms of brassicas and those we've made our own. But grasping for this moment of origin, it becomes clear that nothing in our history is quite so tidy. To this date, researchers remain uncertain of whether the wild brassicas I see as weeds are, indeed, wild at all. Whether they stem from us and have merely grown feral in their escape from our care.

I was a strange child, with a palate more accustomed to bitterness than sweetness. I would ask my mother to cook me Brussels sprouts—sautéed with butter and shallots and cooking sherry—but rarely wanted desserts. In adolescence, I craved rapini, a wilder cultivar of *Brassica rapa*. Gai lan, salty and oil-slick, perfumed with garlic. I'd sit, aged twelve, at our glass dining table, eating bitter greens with bread.

In adulthood, I've grown particularly fond of cabbage. Every few weeks I cross the busy road by my home to buy a flat pale-green head from my local Turkish grocer. One is enough to last me a while, keeping well in the fridge as I slice into it like a loaf of bread. At the shop, the sign tells me it is a Turkish cabbage. But this is a cabbage I know as Taiwanese. Slightly sweet, not round but subtly dome-shaped, with tight, compact leaves. I take it home and cut it into thick wedges, softening it with salt, oil, and heat, with garlic and with chilli. I eat cabbage on its own by the bowlful on weekend afternoons, thinking of other places: of Taipei, where my auntie cooks me fried cabbage with goji berries. Of Canada and the tender braised cabbage with shitakes that my mother cooks when I visit. This is peasant food, she always says, but I cannot think of any vegetable more joyous, more versatile, richer with memory than a cabbage.

When I was twenty-seven, my mother took me to Taiwan's National Palace Museum to see a sculpture more valued than any other. It was a quiet morning, so we could stand in the dim-lit hall alone, looking at the sculpture suspended in its display. Carved by an unknown artist in the nineteenth century, it was once part of the imperial collection in the Forbidden City. Transported to Taiwan in the 1940s, it is now considered an object of vital heritage not just to Taiwan, but across a Chinese diaspora. Tour buses heave open at the museum famous for this piece of jade, and crowds gather to peer into its display case. In the gift shop, replicas of the sculpture are sold as magnets, as keychains. A piece of white and green jade less than twenty centimetres long. It is a sculpture of a cabbage.

One summer in Berlin, I planted a communal garden with my neighbours. We'd been suggesting things to grow in our house WhatsApp group, and I'd drawn up a shortlist. I picked out Grünkohl as one of the crops we should grow in our shared vegetable patch. Grünkohl has long been a German staple, well before kale became trendy. It is sold in bags so enormous—the size of a toddler is a good reference—that not once in the six years I lived there did I manage to fit one in my refrigerator, let alone actually finish one. And it is one of the first German vegetable words I learned—a whole lesson of my German studies in university was devoted to the ways it is typically eaten, boiled with sausages or chopped finely into stews. So choosing it felt like an act of assimilation, an attempt at showing my German neighbours I really could fit in.

To my surprise, one of my younger neighbours told me she didn't find it terribly exciting. She preferred American kale—she said it in English, to distinguish the soft green leaves from the tougher, curlier-leaved varieties of German Grünkohl—and hoped we might plant that instead. Its leaves were more tender, she told me. Kale was generally seen as cooler. And really, I shouldn't have been surprised: the plants we call crops are always bound up with culture—a link not just to land but to the languages, identities, and nations that have created them, prized them, and passed them down. And as much as plants come to stand in for culture, they don't stand still. The borders we draw between cultures and crops have always been more fluid than we can imagine.

Brassicas, then, tell a story of care and entanglement, but also a story of our human cultures. They show us not solely how we have reshaped the wild, and the wild *us*, but the ways our peoples, languages, and literatures have travelled across continents: from the Mediterranean to Eastern Europe, from the Fertile Crescent along the Silk Road, to a contemporary lust for kale chips.

It can be easy to forget that the crops we cook and eat daily were once wild things. Field mustard and wild cabbage grow plentifully—I search for them on my daily walks through city parks, in roadside verges, and in rough meadows. That we can have so altered them from their original forms is simply testament to the notion that, as Michael Pollan writes in *The Botany of Desire*, plants are "willing partners in an intimate and reciprocal relationship with us."

And this entanglement with plants is not a thing of the past but continues in shape-shifted forms. In the 1990s, a variety of stem broccoli was developed by the Japanese seed company and plant breeder Sakata, crossing gai lan with broccoli. But unlike the slow and measured selection we might have carried out in centuries past, where the journey amongst wildness, domestication, and ferality remains at times opaque, plant breeding in our contemporary age is a different thing.

Like most contemporary cultivars, the crop Sakata developed, known in Japan as "Asparation," is instead treated as an object of intellectual property: marketed in the United States under the registered trademark "Broccolini" and in the United Kingdom as "Tenderstem."

The journey from a crop's wild relative to a trademark might seem vast, but in my daily life I find these greens on the same plate: I stock my fridge with bok choy and Tenderstem, cooking them into curries and imagining, absurdly perhaps, that they find in one another a kind of familiarity. Trademarks may be a cultural curiosity, but as the brassicas show us, so too is much of the natural world.

Once the summer season is near its end, the light waning and the mornings growing colder, I bring in the last of the bolted bok choy. It has grown dry in the summer heat. Just a few weeks ago, the plants were studded with yellow flowers—featherlight and tissue-thin. They resembled almost exactly the photos of wild mustard blooms I've seen in researching this essay, and suddenly the distance between that wild plant and our carefully cultivated bok choy seems minuscule. At night, as I sit with my husband hulling the tiny brown seeds from their pods, I imagine all the possibilities the seeds might contain. I imagine just what, when planted and watered next year, they might grow to be.

9.

Bean

1. To begin with, I buy beans. I look for black soybeans for three weeks before settling on yellow. Order a bag of them, dried and paper-wrapped. A kilogram. When they arrive, I plunge my hand into the bag to feel them, then let each yellow soybean clack upon the others as I withdraw myself from amongst them. I order wheat, the same amount. Nut brown, a dry shine.

Spores are harder to find, but I come across them online and hope for the best. Aspergillus sojae. *It arrives in a white paper envelope, the kind you send letters in. Inside is a tiny pouch, a dime bag really, algae green.*

A collection of jars—as big as I can find—needs to be washed and sterilised. A large pan, too, and spoons and ladles and thermometers. I need salt. And water. And time. A lot of it.

Soy, living in memories. Mine are tied to colour: the burnt-brown gleam of soy sauce on fried rice, the chalk white of milk, the green of a bean balanced between my grandmother's chopsticks. The anise-black broth for stewing eggs.

My grandfather often made tea eggs. They emerged from the pot steaming, thick with spice, dark soy, and fragrant tea. He always served them in a soup bowl, peeled already, the eggs half drowned in their elixir.

On my eleventh birthday, my mother gave me a set of white Calvin Klein pyjamas. It was 1997. I'd wanted them for months. My grandfather placed a bowl of tea eggs on the table, and no sooner had I greedily lifted an egg than it slipped back into the broth, splattering my new pyjamas indelible brown. The letters *CK* stained, splattered over. Every time I wore them after that, I could think only of that moment: the slip, the splash, the regret—fleeting.

It was often like this. It was in food that I first learned about pleasure, and I rushed towards the sensations of eating. I wanted soy milk with the texture of velvet, slightly sweet and beany. I drank it hot before bed, cold in the summer, out of Tetra Pak juice boxes on long journeys. I wanted tofu: crisp and salted or deep-fried into puffs, swollen with garlic sauce. Wobbling blocks of bean curd, which Mom would cube and cook with Chinese noodles for weekend lunches.

My life with soy began with desire. And I gave little

thought to the bean at the centre of this story. In the forms I knew it—as tofu, as sauce, as brittle gold sheets of dòu-fupí used for wrapping parcels of mushroom and bamboo, as milk, and as comfort—it seemed to have nothing to do with the yellow-green fields stretching beyond our suburb, across southern Ontario.

The wild soybean's route to domestication remains obscure and contested, tied to nationalist claims from both China and Korea. But this much we can say: in the region where northeastern China meets the Korean peninsula, some three to five thousand years ago, a bushy, twining plant with pale flowers and fuzzy pods became prized for its ability to improve soil. In the staple trinity of local diets—soy, millet, wheat—the beans worked a kind of magic: as fertiliser, protein, sauce, milk, and grain.

Soy subsequently became entwined with culture, health, and imagination for nearly every culture across Asia. In the *Shī jīng*, the Chinese *Classic of Poetry* (1046–761 BCE), the bean is the subject of verse: "They gather the beans, they gather the beans, in their baskets, square and round." In the scraps of what remain of a poem by Song dynasty poet Su Dongpo, blocks of tofu are likened to white jade, and in the lines of Ming dynasty poet Sun Zuo, pools of soy pulp become snow. Over the past three thousand years, a handful of odes to tofu have been written, as well as medicinal tracts on the virtues of soybean porridge, of fermented bean paste, and their derivative sauces. Soy became synonymous with bounty, with the ability to feed oneself, one's livestock, and one's land.

The Japanese Shintō story of Ukemochi no Kami tells of when the Sun Goddess sent her brother, the Moon God, to visit Ukemochi no Kami, the Goddess of Food. She welcomed him, producing a feast from her body: rice, fish, and meat disgorged from her mouth. But insulted that she'd presented him with regurgitated food, the Moon God killed her. And from her body sprouted all the staple foods: millet from her eyebrows, rice from her belly, and from her genitals, soy.

Soybeans were linked to life itself.

2. I gather instructions from as many places as possible; I find surprisingly few. There are books written by men in Nordic countries who love fermentation; YouTube videos of Chinese homemakers; short documentaries about artisanal producers. A few obsessives on the r/fermentation subreddit. The man who sold me the spores also sends instructions.

The first thing they all agree on is to weigh and soak the beans. I weigh them dry and weigh out an equal amount of wheat. I cover the beans generously with water. Let them soak and swell as I sleep.

The next task calls for heat. I boil the beans. Toast the wheat. When cooked, the beans submit to the pressure of finger against thumb. The wheat pops and dances in the pan. When it is cool, I grind it into a fine powder.

The beans—once mixed with the wheat and cooled to forty degrees Celsius—await "inoculation." This sounds serious, but it is simple: I sprinkle the tiny sachet of spores over top. Cover it with a cloth and loose cling film. And wait.

I let days pass. Remembering that a temperature of thirty-five degrees or higher will spoil the batch. My thermometer alarm beeps every so often, when the beans get too warm. I stir fresh air through them. And wait.

In four days, yellow turns to green. A thick shell of mould encases each bean—this means they are ready. Ready to be scooped into sterile jars. For salt, hot brine. To be stirred, daily for the first month. Then weekly for the next. After that, I can leave them unstirred for a month at a time. The longer, some say, the better.

I write a label and date it. Leave the jars in the sunlight, because I read somewhere that sunlight helps. I am not sure if any of this is correct—and I will not know for at least a year. I wait.

Fifteen years ago, I asked my grandmother to tell me about her childhood. So much had gone unspoken; we didn't want to ask her about Nanjing and what she'd endured there during the war. After that, she'd left China and her family in 1949, fled to Taiwan, and had never been able to return.

She was often angry, and that often scared us.

But I realised I knew next to nothing about her: nothing of her family or the ground out of which she'd grown in this world. So one afternoon, I set up a recorder and asked my mother to help translate. We sat around her smoked glass dining table, sipping tea. It was then that I learned that my grandmother's family—amongst other things—had once been manufacturers of soy sauce. That soybeans were at the heart of our family: not simply as flavour and depth in our dishes, but as an income that sustained my ancestors' livelihoods.

My grandmother described girlhood visits to the factory and its outdoor courtyard, lined with rows of enormous clay urns filled with fermenting beans. Each topped with a wicker lid and set out under the southern sun. "They were so heavy it took two men to lift them," she said, miming their motions with frail arms. I imagined the urns my mother kept in the garden, the urns she filled with lilies and water.

I wondered then what smells my grandmother might have known, what flavours. She told me she'd looked on impatiently at beans growing rich with mould atop woven trays, peered beneath the lids of the urns to glimpse the beans at work. Did she count the months before the beans fermented into salted elixir?

How did the sauce they made taste? How deep a brown was its colour?

That soy is central to Chinese life and culture is reflected in language. In Mandarin, when it comes to 黃豆 (huángdòu, yellow bean) it's often enough to simply say 豆 (dòu, bean). In the character, I can see it: a pot and a lid, the beans inside. The words for "soy milk"—豆漿 or 豆奶 (dòujiāng or dòunǎi)—simply mean bean pulp or bean milk. "Tofu" is simply 豆腐 (dòufu, beancurd). Where other beans are identified by their colour—綠豆 (lǜdòu, green/mung bean) or 紅豆 (hóngdòu, red/azuki bean)—the soybean stands as the meaning and measure of a bean.

The word in English is a product of colonial expansion. "Soy" and "soya" come from the Dutch "soja," which is taken from 醬油 (shōyu), the Japanese word for soy sauce. The Dutch held trading posts in Japan and across East Asia from the seventeenth to the nineteenth centuries, acquiring along with territory new foods, methods of production, and words.

The beans themselves took a long time to reach North

America and Europe. Interest in soy began to grow at the end of the nineteenth century, but this didn't mean a boom in tofu or miso production in the West.

Instead, soybeans found themselves caught up in the rapid acceleration of this new century—its trade and its wars. They entered global trade in 1908, driven by the growing market for oil crops. Oil crops were used in the manufacture of industrial lubricants, soap, margarine, cosmetics, lecithin (an emulsifier), and more. This early soy trade emerged in the wake of external pressures on Manchuria, where most of the beans were grown, from both Russian and Japanese imperialism in the region at the turn of the century. By the time soy reached the West, it was through transactions mostly facilitated by Japanese agents.

In 1917, when the United States Department of Agriculture sent their plant explorers in search of a soybean suited for American farms on an industrial scale, Yamei Kin—the Chinese American scientist who led the USDA's efforts to popularise soy—was amongst them. By 1920, the USDA had grown and experimented with up to five hundred varieties of the plant, with some fifteen being commercially available in the United States. In the 1930s, Henry Ford opened a soybean research laboratory to craft plastics, car frames, and trunks from soybeans, spurring the growth of the crop as a promising solution to industrial needs. During the Second World War, when shortages of glycerine-rich tropical oils needed for explosives led to restrictions on their use in manufactured foodstuffs, soy oil stepped in to fill the gap. After that, soy importing and processing in Europe and the United States expanded hugely. And cultivation in the United States increased so much that by the end of the war more soy was grown on home soil than anywhere else, a status that remains unchanged to this day. By 2018, 94 percent of these U.S.-grown soybeans were genetically modified.

Soy in the West has thus been inextricably linked to the technological imaginaries of the twentieth century: as an object of processing, as a crop selected and modified, as myriad nonculinary uses, what historian Ines Prodöhl calls "soy's Americanization." Soy meant oil and animal fodder. Margarine and soap. So it was that soy remained, in many ways, in the background of everyday culinary use—invisible to so many who in fact used the beans daily. These soybeans, stripped of their vitality somehow, seem a far cry from the food so central to Chinese poetry and Japanese legends. So far from the food on my family's table.

In an essay on the pleasures of 豆花 (dòuhuā, tofu pudding), Nina Mingya Powles writes that "The Cambridge Dictionary definition of tofu reads: 'a soft, pale food that has very little flavour but is high in protein, made from the seed of the soya plant.' I feel sad for the person who wrote this." This is soy as but a shadow of itself, soy through the lens of those who cannot see what families like mine have known for centuries.

Kin, in her work with the USDA, was renowned for her abilities with soy: creating ferments and sauces, milks, puddings, cakes, and more. But that Western eaters have repeatedly positioned tofu as bland is a product of concentrated efforts to render this precious food unappealing. It didn't have to be this way. In a 1912 American farmer's exploration of the virtues of soybeans as livestock feed, it is noted that they aren't likely to be grown as human food in the West because "their flavor . . . does not appeal to Caucasian tastes." In the 1920s, German oil mills processed soy in huge quantities—separating oil from the "soy cake" that was turned into livestock feed. Prodöhl writes that "consuming soybeans in an Asian manner—in tofu, for example—would have meant an end to separating the oil from the protein." And so these mills actively shaped the public image of soy through advertising: in one brochure, to protect their trade, they cast tofu and other Asian soy foods, which used the whole bean, as both inconvenient and unpalatable to Europeans.

Over the past two decades, Western dietary advice and xenophobia have too often crossed currents. While soy gained popularity as a cholesterol-free, nutrient-rich source of protein, campaigners against it framed it as a dangerous "propaganda food": from 2007 to 2008, a flurry of news articles probed the question of whether eating soy would induce homosexuality, whether the oestrogen levels of the bean would shrink men's penises. Following a series of problematic but well-publicised studies, the bean was cast as a source of all manner of ailments, from Alzheimer's to breast cancer. That these studies had low sample sizes and often did not differentiate between highly processed soy (as in additives or powders) and whole or fermented foods gave sceptics little pause. The rumours cut across racial and gender lines, built on stereotypes and patriarchal fears: dairy advocates argued that Asians were short because they drank soy instead of cow's milk, while some in the cattle industry worried publicly that the amount of oestrogen contained in the beans might effeminise unsuspecting boys and cause "sexual confusion." In alt-right parlance, a "soy boy" is an effeminate weakling; real dairy stands in for racial and sexual purity.

The gap in framing and flavour between this crop— for in the West "crop" seems an apt term—and the cream-sweet soy I know from childhood is wide. For many years, I sensed it but could not describe it: Why Silk wasn't at all what I knew soy milk to be (a subject meticulously unpacked by Clarissa Wei in her essay "How America Killed Soy Milk"); why when "health-conscious" friends adhering to meat-heavy fad diets tried to warn me off tofu, it felt more like a microaggression than it did concern for my well-being. Why eating soy, at times, has felt like the most powerful expression of my family's identity.

Soy sauce, tofu, and soy milk are foods that take time, but they do not demand enormous knowledge or skill. I have learned from recipes online. Making them offers a kind of solace.

From the apartments I've lived in over recent years—Berlin, London, Cambridge—I watch videos of Li Ziqi, the Chinese vlogger who farms her grandmother's land in rural Sichuan. I watch her, dressed in traditional clothing, carrying baskets into the green. Harvesting soybeans in the field. Freeing them from their fuzzy green pods. Grinding them into a cream-coloured pulp. Thinking about soy, for me, has become a kind of dreaming.

In the past sixteen years, I have moved house more times than I can count, moved countries and continents. Now, in my midthirties, I simply want time and space. As much as I have wanted a child or a family, I've wanted to learn to make soy sauce. I do not know if the skill is in my bones. If my palate is sharp enough to measure the nuances of fermentation. If I will ever be in one place long enough to begin the process and see it through, but I decide to make it anyway.

I tell my husband of my secret dreams: to open a soy-milk shop, a breakfast stall. To open a tofu factory. A soy sauce shop.

I won't, I don't expect—but others have done, will do. I find boutique tofu shops opening in the cities I love, making tempeh and natto from local pulses. Artisanal soy sauce vendors and soy concept stores on the streets of cool neighbourhoods I can no longer afford. Suddenly, unexpectedly, even though so much about soy feels unresolved.

While I write, I soak beans. They swell and burst in their hours of submersion. I boil them, pulse them, strain them for milk. I've learned to make something that replicates that childhood comfort. I sip it warm, fresh from the stove.

A year from now, I will strain sauce from the soy. I'll stack a cast-iron pan, a pestle and mortar, a heavy board atop the fermented mash. I'll leave it overnight and through the morning. The muslin lining the colander will stain a copper brown that shines beneath my kitchen's fluorescent bulb. Everything will have the smell and feel of salt. It'll take a day at least to press the liquid through. A year and five days from when I unpacked dried beans.

For so long, I've dreamt of a home where I can fill jars with soybeans. Just to stir them every day, week, month. Until one day I could lift the lid and witness something—a scent, a flavour—that my grandmother might have known well. The jars of beans my grandmother described to me are long in the distance and the past. But I have sought those sensations still: The grit of salt on bean, the softening of a pulse to pulp. A colour that is far deeper than I can describe.

10.

Sour Fruit

I AM ELEVEN WHEN MY CITRUS OBSESSION BEGINS. It starts with a bag of Minneola tangelos, twelve orange moons in a plastic mesh bag. I've shorn pulp from pith of nine types of citrus at the free samples stall, and the tangelos are the most fragrant. I am not normally a fruit eater—in fact, my parents seem surprised that I am asking to buy the bag of tangelos at all. But these fruits are like nothing I've had before. They melt softly in my mouth, a sharp-sweet sting, and the cloudy membrane around each segment is delicately soft. The sign over their display offers a pseudonym: Honeybells.

The shopfront at Mixon Fruit Farms is fluorescent-lit, with a dusky orange floor and brown wood panelling all around. At the far end of the shop is a soft-serve machine pressing out orange and vanilla swirls. In between, rows of citrus displayed at waist height, the mesh bags coloured to match each fruit. Yellow bags for grapefruits, orange for orange.

I do not know it at the time, but I will have dreams about this shop floor for all of my adult life. The taste of orange and vanilla will always, instantly, return me to this place.

This visit is our annual pilgrimage. Each March, during the school holidays, we catch the tail end of citrus season, in the last weeks before Mixon closes for spring and summer. Back home in Canada, winter is a time of absence; I love the notion of a fruit that arrives only in winter.

The tangelos are amongst the first fruits I can say that I like. I add them to a short list with grapefruits and sour green apples. Until now I have eaten every bitter green that has crossed my plate, but I do not like strawberries, bananas, or kiwis. My mother seems disappointed by this fact. She tells me of the small green oranges in Taiwan, the abundant blood oranges and kumquats. Citrus, I tell her, is something I can love.

Consider the orange: In the early 1990s, citrus groves covered nearly a million acres of Florida, not including the trees that dotted suburban gardens across the state, or the wild citruses that made their homes where they may. But citrus is not native to Florida—it was introduced by the Spanish in the sixteenth century and established itself modestly at first before English colonists led concerted efforts at cultivation in the eighteenth.

I imagine the landscape then—the pines cleared for orange groves.

What could be more Floridian than an orange?

Oranges, any botanist will tell you, come from Northern India, from the Malay Peninsula, from Southern China.

There are some who might see oranges and think of California. Or Spain, perhaps. That is also understandable.

But I think of my mother, teaching me to prise them open with the nail of my index finger, thumbing pith away from tender fruit.

The first citrus trees produced a bitter fruit.

Exactly where and how they hybridised or were domesticated into the fruits we now recognise—mandarin oranges, citrons, pomelos, limes—remains an object of study. One map shows citrus flows across Asia with arrows: citrons bearing west towards India, pomelos southeast, mandarins eastward across China, and limes in nearly all directions, as far as Australia. Their origin point is a red star in western China.

It is the Chinese who are credited with first domesticating oranges many thousands of years ago. The names we use contain a trace of this past: mandarin oranges, and *Citrus × sinensis*, the sweet orange.

In 2018, a group of scientists mapped the genome of the citruses we know today, tracing them back to ten endangered wild species, descended from one long-forgotten Asian ancestor. Our citruses are hybrids derived from two or more of these ten pure species. "Pure" is not a word I have chosen; it is a word I've borrowed from one of the study's co-authors.

The writer Dan Nosowitz describes this process as akin to blending primary colours.

Citrus—by way of trade over land through present-day Iran and Iraq—reached Europe by the time of the Greek author Theophrastus, who described a fruit presumed to be the citron in 310 BCE.

But it was the Spanish, nearly two thousand years later, who brought them over sea to North America. The first

Florida oranges, it is said, were planted in the second half of the sixteenth century. St. Augustine, on the northeastern coast of Florida, was both the oldest colonial city in the United States and, by all accounts, its first orange grove.

I read of how the earliest settlers from Europe planted citrus from the east coast of Canada all the way south to Florida. They assumed similar climatic conditions in North American places to those at the same latitudes in Western Europe. Without the warming winds of the Gulf Stream, crop after crop failed in the cold. But a few groves north of Florida, in Georgia and the Carolinas, flourished nonetheless. Still, we do not often speak of Georgia oranges.

It always surprises me how little humans have understood the living world with which we have made our fortunes.

At Lunar New Year each winter, my family eats mandarin oranges because they symbolise wealth. Gold fruit is a luxury in a cold season.

Before the tangelos, every time I've eaten an orange I've sucked the juice from each vesicle and spat out the skin. I tell my mother I do not like fruits that have texture.

My mother, for whom good fruit is the most valued thing.

She does not say it explicitly, but I know that this pickiness leads her to believe that I am more like my father than I am like her.

The earliest North American citrus trees were planted with the hope of riches. Of course, the fruits had to get to a market—which meant transportation. And a people eager to eat relatively sour oranges.

Citrus thrived in the region across northern Florida accessible by boat along the St. Johns River, and once railroads were established, farther south and westward. The trains opened new markets for citrus in the northern states—and it was after their establishment in the 1880s that historians began to really speak of a citrus industry.

In time, Florida oranges proved themselves to bring good fortune: land under cultivation as citrus groves increased by five times between the end of the nineteenth century and the end of the twentieth, but yields of the fruit increased forty-three times. We might credit pesticides, fertilisers, or hardy root stocks with this transformation.

The fruiting part of the orange we eat—the scion—comes from a nicer-tasting cultivar grafted onto hardier, tougher roots.

"Scion" can mean a graft, shoot, or twig. But it can also mean a descendent of an important family. All the citruses we value were shaped by human hands—are they, too, our descendants?

It is August when Rowan turns up to my thirty-fifth birthday lunch carrying a tree. It is too heavy for her to manage with one hand, so she slides it across the threshold of Emma-Lee's apartment. The tree isn't enormous, but it comes in a pot the size of my torso, soil tightly packed around its root ball. Rowan frowns; I am five months pregnant, and she now wonders how I might carry this orange tree home. I do not mind, because I feel as though she has seen into my heart with this gift.

It isn't exactly an orange tree. But it is a citrus: a long, skinny stem and a green crown, bulbous and studded with flowers shaped like stars. × *Citrofortunella mitis* its label reads—a cross between a tiny tangerine and a kumquat. She has given me a calamansi tree.

Rowan tells me that she asked the shopkeeper for a tree that would grow in Taiwan, because my mother is from there. The calamansi is considered native to the Philippines, with a range reaching Taiwan and Southern China at its northern limit, Indonesia to the south.

I am asking this tree to live in a garden in England.

The USDA launched the first formalised citrus breeding programme in the world in Florida in 1893. Most breeding served to develop varieties hardier against the cold, more suitable for transport, more resistant to pests. But making oranges more widely palatable was also one aim of these efforts.

USDA plant physiologist Walter Tennyson Swingle bred the first tangelo—a cross between a tangerine and a grapefruit—in 1897. One hundred years before I ate one and decided that I liked it.

Swingle—who according to one history of Florida citrus had never seen an orange tree before being posted to the USDA's centre in Florida—would spend his formative years working on citrus and some years as a USDA plant explorer. But alongside this work on plants, he began to collect classics of Chinese literature: botanical and medicinal texts, geographic treatises, gazetteers. Swingle would guide the acquisition of East Asian texts for the U.S. Library of Congress for many decades, helping the library amass more than one hundred thousand volumes. The Western science of botany, he would contend, required attention to the knowledge that had preceded it.

Though I did not know it at the time, it is through Swingle's work that I've encountered so many texts central to the history of botany and my family's Chinese heritage. I do not often find synchronicity in the world, but it feels significant that I've learned his name.

The Minneola tangelo, named for a city in central Florida, was released by Swingle in 1931. To create it, he crossed a Duncan grapefruit with a Dancy tangerine.

Swingle described the tangelo in sensuous terms: "greenish in cross section; pulp of orange color (Ridgway, mikado orange), translucent, tender, melting, very juicy, somewhat aromatic, combining desirable sweetness and acidity."

I am reminded that plant taxonomy is not a great distance from poetry.

A year after I first taste the Minneola tangelo, 1998, an Asian citrus psyllid arrives on a jasmine plant in a garden in the south Florida city of Boynton Beach. Its arrival sparks concern; the psyllid native across Asia is a known vector of a disease called citrus greening.

This is also the year my mother is refused service in a bank in Savannah, Georgia, as we drive from Florida to Canada. They serve my father instead. It is the first time I hear him call someone "a racist."

More often than not, citrus greening is referred to by its Chinese name: "huánglóngbìng" (黃龍病)—yellow dragon disease—or "HLB" for short. Originally, it was named "huáng*lung*bìng" (黃梢病), yellow shoot disease, in the local Guangdong dialect where it was first named. The phonic change is understandable; when a disease is so devastating, wouldn't we rather attribute it to a dragon?

The small brown psyllid—just four millimetres long at its largest—was found across Florida within a matter of years. By 2005, the presence of huánglóngbìng caused by the psyllid was confirmed in Miami. Today, all citrus-producing counties in Florida are impacted by this disease.

Its impact is felt in citrus-producing regions across the world: in China, the Philippines, Mexico and Central America, and in East Africa especially.

When a tree has huánglóngbìng, its vascular system degrades. The fruit that does grow is smaller, sourer, and remains eternally green, even when ripened. Citrus greening cannot be cured, and within a few years, the tree will die.

Why have I asked you to consider the orange? This is an essay I've titled "Sour Fruit," though I am writing of a fruit I found sweet.

In the past ten years, scholars across the sciences and humanities have grappled with the notion of the Anthropocene, arguing that our geologic era is best described by our human transformation of the natural world. But a group of anthropologists have put forward another suggestion to help us understand how the world has changed: "Plantationocene."

In the Plantationocene, systems of cultivation, global transport, enslavement, plant transfers, and power characterise our era. Most often, scholars point to sugar, cotton, and other crops deeply tied to slave labour in the Americas.

But oranges, as the historian Tiago Saraiva contends, might also teach us something of uneven power in this world.

Saraiva traced clones of California oranges through cultivation in Palestine by Jewish settlers and by French colonists in Algeria and Morocco to their influence on Frantz Fanon's *The Wretched of the Earth*. By understanding how crops like oranges have moved, been cultivated, thrived, and declined, we see not just a history of a plant species but our own social, political, scientific histories, too.

In citrus there is an echo that asks: Who makes this crop possible?

In 1945, one T. Ralph Robinson wrote in a history of Florida citrus: "The labor of picking and packing has gradually passed to migrant workers, and the effect may be seen in the decline of some of our rural communities."

In 2002, three Florida citrus producers were sentenced to prison for enslaving some seven hundred undocumented migrant workers.

Less than twenty years on from the first case of huánglóng-bìng in Florida, output of citrus has dropped 80 percent. In

2022—following devastating hurricanes and the impact of disease—it reached lows not seen since the 1940s.

Occasionally, plant breeders seeking sweeter fruit happen upon unintended—but positive—outcomes: a 2009 cross between mandarins and Minneola tangelos has produced an orange called the Sugar Belle. Only once it was cultivated did researchers realise it is tolerant to huánglóngbìng.

But research takes more time than many have.

This year, I read that Mixon, where I first tasted the Minneola tangelo, is up for sale. The farm has already reduced from 350 acres to just 50. In 2018, they tried diversifying by planting bamboo. I try to picture it: a future in which Florida is not famous for oranges, but for bamboo shoots.

It isn't like my memory of the place. But I know that little remains unchanged.

It is January. The windows of the conservatory have fogged, and my breath puffs white ahead of me. Stepping into the garden—where frost has covered the entire green world in flecks of ice—I realise I've forgotten about the calamansi tree. I'd meant to bring it indoors last night, my neighbour having warned me about the freeze. Its leaves are covered in pale silver film, crisper than they were the day before. The tight flower buds have turned from white to beige. The fruits chartreuse to yellow. It isn't too late, I know—a day or two in the relative warmth of the conservatory might just do to save the tree and speed its ripening along.

A tree whose parent plant, the kumquat, was given its botanical name by one Walter Tennyson Swingle.

When Lunar New Year comes, my mother is visiting. I buy two net bags of mandarins, which we peel and eat at the dining room table. The fruit is too sweet, its membranes too dry. I discreetly drop the chewed skin from my mouth into a napkin.

It has been twenty years since I've seen a Minneola tangelo. It isn't a fruit I ever find outside of Florida or outside of my childhood.

On the second day of the Lunar New Year, I pluck three ripe fruits from the calamansi tree. They are no larger than marbles, the pores on their waxy skin no bigger than pinpricks. My mother does not believe me when I tell her we can eat them—they look too small and sad from an English winter, perhaps. Still, I slice them across with a small knife.

I ask my mother to open her mouth. I squeeze what juice I can from this sour fruit.

At the Scale of Water Drops

IN AN ESSAY TITLED "ARTS OF INCLUSION, OR HOW to Love a Mushroom," the anthropologist Anna Tsing documents the ways one might see a mushroom as kin. She speaks to a herbarium curator, considers the history of fungal taxonomy, gleans the history of the matsutake mushroom from conversations with pickers and researchers. Fundamentally, she concludes, it is through *noticing* connections with other species—specifically, noticing mushrooms—in an indeterminate way.

I first read this essay when I was in graduate school, curled up at a wooden table with my laptop balanced on my knees. I'd been reading essay after essay on new materialism, multispecies ethnography, the ways a blurry knowledge of quantum physics could upend just about every humanities discipline. Tsing's essay—along with another in which she gives voice to a mushroom spore travelling the globe—stood out to me. Not because I was all that interested in fungi, but because I had for a long time struggled with what noticing nature might look like.

I didn't grow up with a knowledge of local plants, though I certainly grew up with gardens and the introduced species they gather into them. As a result, it wasn't until adulthood that I even began properly learning which trees were which, or the names of wildflowers, or the songs of birds. I didn't think of myself as particularly good at classifying or *knowing things* about nature so much as I felt drawn simply to natural beauty. So this call to notice details in nature without necessarily categorising—and not just the charismatic flora easily grasped by eye, but the smaller scales, too—felt particularly inviting to me.

I was drawn to mosses. Mosses don't grow all that plentifully where I grew up. But once I moved to Britain, my eye was consistently attracted to green: green growing on the railings, on the brick walls of terraced houses, in clumps on roof slates, and occasionally at the edges of the pavements. Moss needs moisture, and that was plentiful. What else was easily noticed yet so often neglected? I did a Google search for the science of mosses, liverworts, and hornworts—"bryology"—and saw that it was autocorrected to "biology."

Mosses are notoriously hard to identify in the field. For this reason, there were no bryologists on the botany course I took, and we spent relatively little time discussing their complexities. They told us simply that often more than hand tools are needed to tell mosses apart from one another. We were working with 10x hand lenses for larger plants; the British Bryological Society recommends 20x for working with mosses in the field. In the scope of the course, we didn't have the time or training for microscopes and slides.

Still, I felt a strange kinship and wonder every time I thought about mosses. The evolutionary bridge between life in water and life on land, they are a subtle but omnipresent link to the deep past. The oldest moss fossils we have are dated at 350 million years old, found in the east of Germany, some three hundred kilometres south of Berlin. After flowering plants, bryophytes are the most diverse group of plants, with around twenty thousand species existing today.

But unlike many other land plants, mosses live according to one very strict condition: they are "poikilohydric," meaning that without vascular tissue structure to suck up water from the surrounding area, like other plants do, mosses are at the mercy of their environment. They remain bound to water: to places where moisture is plentiful, or where weather can provide. With tiny leaves just one cell thick, most mosses may lack the ability to grow to the sizes of trees or other herbaceous plants, but they can tuck into tiny cracks, into shaded potholes and gaps unseen. And just as they thrive at the extremes of size, they are able to survive other exceptional states. The same circumstances that leave mosses vulnerable to the environment also enable them to survive extreme fluctuations in conditions: desiccating during periods of drought, waiting during periods of extreme cold. In 2014, researchers with the British Antarctic Survey grew a more-than-1,500-year-old *Chorisodontium aciphyllum* moss sampled from a frozen ice core extracted from the permafrost of Signy Island, a short way off Antarctica. Cryptobiosis—the ability to survive in suspended animation—is a curious possibility for a moss.

It was after learning all this that I began trying to know the mosses I encountered. I was not a bryologist—certainly not even that good at identification—but I wanted to practice what Tsing called the art of noticing. I wanted, as Robin Wall Kimmerer suggests, to learn to see in a way that was more like listening. Once I could really see them, I could begin to learn their names.

The mosses I encountered in the forests around Berlin were all fairly common. I found *Mnium hornum*—swan's-neck thyme moss—on a trail north of the city. A beginner's moss, its deep green leaves shone bright at the site of new growth, and its spore capsules hung clustered like streetlamps over soft ground. I found *Dicranum scoparium*—broom fork moss—with its pointed leaves. I brushed my hands against it and it felt like feathers. I tried to notice all their details. But at this tiny scale, I found it difficult to commit them to memory.

And then I found a moss I could not forget. I was south of Berlin, in a section of trails that cut through the patchwork of heathland and forest between the lakes. Here the ground often grew sandy and bare where tree cover let up. The moss formed dense, dark carpets of matte green, appearing fuzzy from a distance. Up close, each of its tiny leaves crescendoed to a point. Fine filamentous hairs emerged from each, so that this tiny plant had the look of a fountainous firework, an exploding star. *Campylopus introflexus*, I read, was often called heath star moss. I found this name enchanting, immediately filing it in my mind as a moss I would remember. What I didn't know then was that heath star moss is also one of the world's most notorious invasive species.

In April 1941, British botanist John Braybrooke Marshall recorded an occurrence of a carpet-like moss on a sandy, stony slope in Sussex, in the southeast of England. Growing olive green, it sat between heather and birches. Marshall sampled the moss and recorded it as *Campylopus introflexus*. First described in 1801 by Johann Hedwig—who called it *Dicranum introflexum*—this was a moss described as local to "Insularum meridionalium" (the southern isles). Today it is understood as native to temperate South America, Southern Africa, Australia, Aotearoa New Zealand, and the Subantarctic Islands.

Before 1941, heath star moss had already been recorded throughout Britain, particularly along the Cornwall coast, with records dating back to 1829. This had led to the widespread belief that this moss had a cosmopolitan range, growing not just in the Southern Hemisphere but also in Europe, albeit often in different conditions. But the example Marshall found growing in Sussex, and that others soon began recording across England, Wales, Scotland, and Ireland, were conspicuously distinct from those seen growing in Britain before: it was a large example, akin to a carpet, while others had previously been spotty. And this moss seemed to spread more readily. Before 1941, *Campylopus introflexus* hadn't been recorded in Britain in its sporulating stage.

So bryologists began to consider the notion that, before 1941, the moss they'd been recording hadn't actually been *Campylopus introflexus* at all. In 1955, after comparing specimens, botanist V. Giacomini determined it was a distinct species—more prone to growing on undisturbed, rocky shorelines—now known as *Campylopus pilifer* or stiff swan's-neck thyme moss. Which meant that the appearance of heath star moss, plentiful and spreading across disturbed, acidic, burned, or eroded ground, without a known source of introduction, was worth noticing.

As bryologists began recording it across Britain and continental Europe, they observed it thriving near ports along the temperate Atlantic coast and moving steadily inland and eastward. Due to its rapid spread, some conjectured that the species had been dispersed across the continent by tanks during the Second World War—though the timeline means this compelling explanation is doubtful—resulting in another common name for the species: tank moss. By 1954, the "tank moss" was recorded in France, by 1961 in the Netherlands, and by 1967 in Germany.

More likely, heath star moss spread efficiently by spore, dispersing by wind over vast distances of the European landscape. In 1975 it was recorded in North America on a gravel roof in Arcata, California—though a recent account offers specimens collected as early as 1967 and 1971 in Northern California—and from there it began to spread in a similar fashion, at a similar rate along the West Coast. Its current nonnative range extends from as far north as Iceland, south to the Mediterranean. Across Russia, North America's Pacific coast, and Western Europe. As it colonised new ground, it began to dominate in coastal dunes and heathlands, its thick carpet quickly crowding out other species. On heathlands in particular, where the star moss grew thick, heather struggled to regenerate. Local species usually engaged in the process of succession—where plants colonise bare ground to eventually form grasslands, shrubs, and forests—could not compete where the heath star moss took hold.

Once I began looking for it, I realised how widely distributed heath star moss actually is. On the National

Biodiversity Network Atlas, I browsed occurrences of the species across Great Britain. The records are verified by name and whether the source has been accepted. Each has coordinates marking the spot and a note of its rough location. On the map, entries are marked by a red dot in a green square, visible only once I'd zoomed in close to each place. I began to imagine the moments of these encounters. I looked at London and saw a scattering of dots in places I know well. On Hampstead Heath, near the edges of the western ponds. One old record placed it in the patch of marshy land I walked near daily when we lived in East London, between the railway lines that cut across Walthamstow and Lea Bridge. It was recorded on Jesus Green, by the lock on the River Cam, and in Richmond Park, where I once carried out field survey training, gathering grass species from quadrants between deer-browsed trees. At Holkham Beach, where my husband and I spent a last weekend away before becoming parents, I saw that it lives scattered amidst the dunes and shaggy pines of the North Norfolk coast.

The more I read of the moss, the more I struggled to connect the enchantment I first felt upon encountering it with the words so often used to describe it: "alien," "exotic," "invasive." I read studies of the species with titles that seem more akin to sci-fi B-movies—"Invasion of the Alien Moss"—and began to think of the other species that might have been thriving were it not for this vigorous, beautiful moss. I realised quickly how my thinking about mosses had been shaped by their diminutive size. The words I was most likely to use in describing them, like "tiny," "wondrous," or even "cute," dispelled my own understanding of their force and impact on the world. In my own enchantment—because mosses are small—I had stripped them of so much of the power they hold.

Robin Wall Kimmerer describes mosses as "beautifully adapted for life in miniature": thriving on surfaces where other species cannot. Both water and wind make these lives possible. In a chapter on the "boundary layer," she writes of the tiny microclimate in which a moss exists. Lay low to the ground on a windy day and you might feel something like it: the wind speed slowing, the relative warmth granted by the stilled air of the surface. It is this boundary that determines how tall a moss might grow. And it is within this boundary that mosses thrive. Lacking roots, a moss must await the water that allows it to photosynthesise light: mosses, I later hear Kimmerer say on a podcast, are "designed at the scale of water drops." They need water to survive, and water or wind to spread: spores of some species are dispersed as water flows past, while others travel lightly by air. The portrait painted is one of mosses in waiting.

It is generally assumed that heath star moss was brought first to England by people, and that its spread to distant and new environments has largely been facilitated by footfall—that is, the moss very likely made its way to new lands on the soles of our shoes. Birds and other wildlife may also be a vector, as tiny fragments of the moss can become entangled in fur and feather, travelling vast distances at animal scales.

But mosses can be far more agential than all of that. In the case of heath star moss, its rapid dispersal over the European continent has most likely been carried out on its own accord. Think of the term "invasive" and remember that even a tiny moss can be a powerful force in a landscape: a tiny fragment of it may clonally reproduce a genetically identical individual to the plant it came from. Its spores can travel on fast winds over vast distances. Its spread goes largely unnoticed, until suddenly, a carpet of heath star moss is there and thickening.

The impact of heath star moss on the places it grows depends largely on the land itself. In pine forests and plantations, its effects have been viewed as fairly negligible—which is why it isn't considered a particularly serious threat in the landscape I first encountered it, near Berlin. On heathlands and coastal dunes, however, its impact is more pronounced: inhibiting the growth of heather in the former, and forming thick carpets that prevent lichen species from thriving in the latter. Researchers worry for the biodiversity of dunes across northern Europe in particular, as the heath star moss slows not just the growth of lichens that usually would dominate, but seems to outcompete a host of other moss species considered native. At least one account lays blame for the decline of the tawny pipit—a bird listed as threatened in Europe—upon the encroachment of heath star moss.

On a fact sheet on invasive species, I read about the ways researchers have tried to eradicate heath star moss. Herbicide: little impact. Burial in sand: tolerated. Removal: it returns. Burning: it returns. I read that in the Netherlands, where it has had a particularly unwanted impact on dunes, someone is building a machine to remove it. I wonder if it will be of any use. Under "Prevention" I read simply that its dispersal cannot be prevented. Eradication, it says, is impossible.

More than any other I have encountered, this is a species whose movements cannot be held at bay. To do so would require us to think and act beyond a scale to which we are accustomed. We do not know how to live at the scale of a moss fragment. Let alone a spore. How, then, can we learn to live with the heath star moss?

As I read, I came across a photograph of a hillside covered with deep green carpet, cut through with clouds of white smoke. I learned that in Iceland—where the moss appeared via tourism, it is assumed—the species lives only around geothermal vents. This isn't unexpected: in its native range, the moss has been recorded in similar conditions, where little else is able to survive. It has been recorded growing at ground temperatures up to forty-seven degrees Celsius. And this I found compelling: the heath star moss will make a life for itself in a dune, or in a forest, or on a heath, or even a baking, smoking hole in the earth. I never expected a little moss to be this powerful.

Kimmerer writes that mosses experience the world as individual stems, so we too must think at the same tiny scale. But I could not stop thinking of the vastness of heath star moss's world—the way it refuses tininess, or containment, or the sweetness with which I may have liked to imagine it.

I began to look on the map, wanting to see the places this moss holds on to. In the South Sandwich Islands, east of the Falklands, it grows around volcanic vents that dot black specks of land in the sea, presumably distributed by wildlife. Species here grow in concentric rings, arranging themselves by their tolerance for high temperatures, heath star moss leading the way. I looked for pictures of the islands, and found one labelled with place names: Basilisk Peak, Sombre Point. Some distance away, towards Antarctica, I found the moss's southernmost home. It is a curled-up, rocky landmass, akin to a sleeping dog turned nose to tail. A caldera, its volcano still active beneath the sea. Here, on Deception Island, heath star moss lives where the fumaroles provide meagre warmth. Where little else finds a hospitable home, I thought of it finding warm ground at the cold poles of our Earth.

12.

Seed

GIFT

Our first day begins with a seed.

We have travelled over land by train and by ferry, arriving in England from Germany via the Netherlands. The rules are shifting, week to week. Because of the route we have travelled—passing through regions where concentrations of the virus cross a certain threshold—we are required to quarantine. Two weeks in our new flat, looking out at our new street below. We do not know the neighbourhood yet, but from the windows we begin to know its skies.

We've moved back to Britain so I can take on a job thinking about seeds and their stories. I am tied for this time to a research project on the histories and futures of crops, planning visits to sites of crop conservation, assisting other researchers by gathering material from digital archives. I find myself thinking about plants constantly.

Making connections between the work I am doing and the seeds I am planting, the trees I encounter, the fruits and vegetables that I buy.

Shortly after we arrive, while we are still in quarantine, our friends Nina and David drop by. They stay two metres back from the front door, though the dog rushes out to greet them. The dog is not in quarantine, and they have offered to take him for a walk. Before they go, Nina drops a red gift bag marked with the Chinese character 福 (fú) on the doorstep. Upstairs in our west-facing kitchen, I unpack three types of noodles, seaweed-flecked rice crackers, and a paper bundle of soybeans. At the bottom of the bag sits a tiny packet of seeds. I examine the paper envelope and realise she has folded it herself. On the side, she has written in pencil: "marigolds."

Holding the seeds, I feel all the more conscious that I cannot go outside. That I have not yet touched the green hedge beyond our doorway or the skinny trees that line our road. It is autumn, no time to be planting marigolds. But still the seeds have me thinking of soil. I am reminded that the time will come. To hold a seed is to be oriented towards the future.

GRAFT

In winter, a landscaping crew arrives with their truck and chipper. They park next door, in front of the neighbour's apple tree that cascades its branches over our walkway. I've plucked sour apples from the tree to make cider vinegar and nudged the spoiled fruit into the flower beds to decompose. The neighbour does not use the tree, tells me he does not notice it much at all. But I know from sitting by the window watching that the robin does, as do the blue tits. The lichen on its bark knows the tree better than any of us.

The men bring out ladders, clippers, and saws and begin to hack the tree apart. It is not my tree, I know. But I watch from the window. No one watches me, so my devastation feels private. Quiet against the sound of a chainsaw.

In the months before the landscapers came, at work I arranged a team field trip to Brogdale and its National Fruit Collection, a stretch of orchard land in Kent run in partnership with the University of Reading. Apples were in season when we went—and it is apples for which the collection is perhaps best known. A man in a red fleece jacket led our tour, carrying with him no notes, only a pocket knife with which to cut fruit.

Apples, like many fruit trees, are a strange thing. Always original in the seed, a particular variety can be duplicated only by grafting. The apple trees at Brogdale were laid out in tidy rows, all labelled with their variety and a date. The trees were more varied in size than I'd seen before at pick-your-own orchards, with skinny trees draped over stakes and dotted amidst older, bushier specimens. All were heavy with fruit: irregular orbs in dusty orange and burnt yellow. Most of the apples were not the brightly hued varieties common to supermarket shelves, but apples at risk of extinction. Apples once grown and largely forgotten, save to a few enthusiastic heritage fruit growers. Apples collected from every county in Britain, kept alongside cultivars from across the world. The guide led us through the apple orchard, past medlars, quinces, cherries, and plums. Past a poly-tunnel the size of a warehouse, in which researchers are trialling apple varieties to find one that can withstand climate breakdown. And then he let us choose which ones we'd like to try. I lingered over the beauty of their names: Pommersche Krummstiel, Parker's Pippin, Citron d'Hiver, Climax.

The Brogdale collection is a living museum, preoccupied with the possibility of loss. It is only in the presence of possible loss that conservation makes sense. More than two thousand varieties of apple are kept there, and, because of the habit of apple seeds to reinvent themselves, all must be kept as trees.

At my window, I am still watching as the workers toss branches of the neighbour's apple tree into the chipper, sending flakes of the wood all over. They begin raking debris from the roadside. I sit down to work but still watch from my desk. Thinking only of the seeds of those apples, the longing for life they held, and all the newness they might have produced. Eventually, the workers stop, reload their truck, and drive away. I remain where I am, stunned in the silence, staring at a cup where I am storing scissors and pens. Inside is the envelope of marigold seeds.

GENE

With the seeds on my desk, I begin the task of cataloguing histories of European crop databases, asking how early collections of seeds were documented, maintained, and shared. The lead researcher I am working with, Helen Anne Curry, has asked me to gather accounts of crop conservationists in the 1970s, 1980s, 1990s, and 2000s. I read scans of institutional reports, calling for plant genetic resources to be better preserved and organised. I read of efforts to share those resources, of the need for standardised databases on European collections of barley varieties, on peas, alliums, and stone fruits.

The early databases I am researching emerged in a period of acute concern for the loss of plant biodiversity across the globe. While in the mid-twentieth century a "Green Revolution" promised improved and standardised crop varieties designed by plant breeders, the concomitant industrialisation of agriculture led to fears that the broader diversity of plants in our world might be lost. Add to that worries of Cold War destruction, and by the 1960s and '70s an international drive to collect, record, and safely store the genetic heritage of the world came to dominate conservation. Huge numbers of seeds were gathered, but they were often stored or recorded in inconsistent ways, with

duplicates unchecked. Streamlining the seed-banking process was not only necessary to make the collections actually
useful to plant breeders hoping to access the genetic diversity they held, but was, I learn from Helen, an essential
component of care for genetic material viewed as a global
patrimony.

Today, visions of seed banks differ vastly from these
early collections. There are some 1,700 seed banks in this
world—from small facilities that house their collections
in situ to the vast, technologically minded complexes that
promise secure stewardship of the planet's genetic diversity. These are seed banks recast as vaults that harken
back to Cold War fears; Kew's Millennium Seed Bank at
Wakehurst is housed in an underground bunker that is
bomb-, flood-, and radiation-proof. It holds more genetic
diversity than any site in the world: nearly all of Britain's
native plants are banked as seed, as well as seeds from
ninety-seven other countries. The Svalbard Global Seed
Vault—which styles itself as "the ultimate insurance policy for the world's food supply"—is carved into the permafrost of Longyearbyen, on a Norwegian island north of the
Arctic Circle. Housing millions of duplicates of other seed
bank collections from across the globe, it is "the backup of
the backup," Helen tells me. Seed banks exist in orientation
towards an uncertain future, but their existence remains
deeply linked to the particularities of a twentieth-century
world.

It is impossible to understand the seed bank in isolation from the context of imperialism. The existence of the Millennium Seed Bank grew out of the needs of a nation facing its empire's decline. In the course of my work, I come across Xan Chacko, who has studied Kew's seed-banking practices up close. She argues that their creation of a cold-storage seed bank served to rebrand the longstanding extraction of plants and seeds from former colonies under the frame of conservation. And that if we are to understand the role of the Millennium Seed Bank now, we need to understand the context out of which it emerged.

When the idea for the Seed Bank was first proposed, government agencies were initially reticent to fund such a vast facility. It would be enormously expensive, and the ideological reasons for doing so were not yet clear. But seed banking, Chacko argues, has always been tied to nation: the subsequent spread of Dutch elm disease across Britain—marring the beauty of the cherished national landscape—quickly underscored the need to protect native flora, and the project was thus approved. Opened in 2000, the seed bank named for the new millennium could be seen in contrast to the historic legacy of the Botanic Garden, opened in 1759 as a site of colonial authority over nature. At the height of its empire, Britain held a quarter of the world's territory. Today, the Millennium Seed Bank holds more than 10 percent of all the plant species on Earth.

Seed banks do not reach this scale at random. Whether

a seed is collected at all is shaped by its tolerance to cold storage, its vulnerability to climate change, its rarity, and most crucially, its utility to humans. We do not insure what we do not value; but how we decide what is worth saving is tied deeply to where and when we make that calculus.

When I begin researching the European crop databases, my knowledge of seed banks is little more than fascination with the work they carry out: as spaces of conservation, as spaces of deep care for plants. I am excited about the idea of a seed bank—because of the promise of conservation the idea entails. But the language I encounter asks me to think differently, and in abstraction. In the language of seed banking, it is not the plant that is stored, but its potential: not a seed, but "germplasm," a seed framed as genetic possibility. Seeds in the seed bank become "accessions," like files in an archive. In order to be useful in abstraction, every collection needs a standardised system for managing accessions: with dates, with places, names, and descriptions. It can be difficult to put into words the exact conditions from which a seed was collected—a valley perhaps, with a certain type of soil, a certain community of stewardship. To bank a seed in the Doomsday Vault, as Svalbard is sometimes called, is to house its genetic material in abstraction from the specific lifeworld in which it arose— as accessions we hope never to have to use.

But much as we extract a seed from its environment, it remains a very material relic of a plant from the past. It carries the record of the climate before it was collected in how well it responds to drought, fire, or floods. Critics of ex situ seed banking (that is, storing seeds away from their original environment) note that removing a seed from an environment in which it can evolve in accordance with climate change makes banked seeds less useful in a changing world. And even when they are banked, seeds are not a stable record of the past: as their viability wanes, they must occasionally be grown out into plants that flower and go to seed, so those seeds can be reharvested and stored again. Svalbard, Helen writes, becomes "a site from which to restore copies rather than warehouse originals." And copies are not always entirely faithful to their originals.

This streamlined vision of nature as genetic material effaces the centuries-long relationships amongst plants, people, and places: the role of farmers as stewards of landraces—cultivars developed specifically to the conditions of a particular place over many generations—and the social landscapes from which they arise, a specificity chefs often call terroir. Because in a field or on a hillside, where a plant grows, a different kind of knowledge can exist. How plants interact with the soil, with light, and with rain. The ways some plants thrive together, in the exact conditions of a particular valley where a landrace originated, in the hands of a steward who knows not just that seed but its ancestors, too. In order to believe in seed banking's efficacy, we must on some level believe the seed alone can make up for that loss. We must, to borrow a term from a group of historians of science, be "seed determinists."

As I work, I arrange folders on a digital drive I've shared with other researchers on our team—mirroring the work of the institutions I am learning about. I label them by utility, by year, by topic, and by crop. I am at a great distance from the scent of soil and the sensation of plants growing. But still, in the coldness of cataloguing, I catch sight of human errors: a reduplication, an error in a plant's description. Looking closely, I see that no seed bank can be a perfect abstraction from the lived world.

Before this job, my only encounter with the logic of seed saving was at Kew, where I met two seed curators on a short botany course. They told me how strange it was to be spending time in the herbarium working with plant specimens or out in the field surveying plots when their daily jobs involved working solely with seeds in the laboratory.

In her research on the Millennium Seed Bank, Xan Chacko spent time working with seed curators at the site, documenting the physical and subjective labour that went into producing a collection of its size. Thinking back to the curators I met, and reading Chacko's account, I realise that this is not a labour that can be described as cold. At least part of the labour of seed banking is a deeply intimate act of care.

After seeds are collected in the field—itself an endeavour requiring not just funding but skill, time, and risk—they must be cleaned, screened, and counted. Curators are hired in part based on their manual dexterity, as their work involves stripping tiny seeds of their husks, extracting the part of a plant reduced to germplasm. A curator, working with each individual seed—for each is valuable in a seed bank—might work with a microscope, tweezers, and a scalpel. Seeds might be sieved or sorted by weight in an aspirator. When a seed is clean enough, and whether it is deemed of good-enough quality for banking—all subjective pronouncements on some level—require both individual care and attention. Seed banking requires a belief in a world worth protecting.

A part of me resists the technoscientific faith that Svalbard requires: I think of cryogenic storage and see the image of a man frozen, a sci-fi future from films and stories. In my imagination, I often conflate the seed vault with another, more sinister vault: Onkalo, the deep-underground Finnish repository for nuclear waste designed to last one hundred thousand years. Set nearly five hundred metres into the bedrock, Onkalo is a tomb, designed never to be opened. Onkalo is for whoever may follow in our wake. What we keep in Svalbard—we might vainly hope—should not need to be used. But it was built so that we might use it, in a future that we cling tight to.

And I know that it is necessary even in our present—not solely in response to a threat on the distant horizon but to very real conflicts that persist in our world. In 2015,

ICARDA—a gene bank based originally in Syria—made the first ever withdrawal of seeds from Svalbard. The war in Syria had forced the closure of ICARDA's Aleppo head-quarters, resulting in the loss of its collection specialised to desert environments. By 2019, three withdrawals from Svalbard had restored seeds that would be otherwise ir-replaceable, putting food security in arid environments at risk. At new facilities in Lebanon and Morocco, the seeds are being reproduced once again, reduplicated, and re-turned to storage.

So I may not think of soil when I think of seed banks—but I do think of the past, and the future that the past makes possible. Perhaps a seed's time is not as linear as I imagine it to be.

GIFT

In late January, a year and a half after we move back to Brit-ain, I plant two varieties of tomato and one variety of chilli pepper. One of the tomatoes is from a commercial seed packet—a balcony variety I've successfully grown in con-tainers before—while the other is from a seed-saving ex-change late in the autumn. The tomatoes are blight-resistant Primabellas, and the chilli peppers, which I got from the same place, bear the name Dragon's Tongue.

A few weeks before the last frost, I finally plant the marigold seeds, too, in pots lined up along the west-facing window. I read about their needs: fertile, well-draining soil,

warmth, and generous light. I begin to imagine an unfurling of green leaf, a concentration of energy into blossom.
My garden in yellow and gold. But after two weeks, when
they have not germinated, I begin to worry. Perhaps I've
left the seeds too long, and certainly at the wrong temperature. I look up my problems online: my soil is too damp, the
window too cold. I feel silly, because everything I read tells
me that marigolds should be simple plants to grow. The
internet tells me they are "surefire," "easygoing," that they
ought to grow in almost any soil. I think of Nina's hands,
saving these seeds from the plants grown on her balcony,
and think of the labour that went into collecting them. I
think of the many hands, scalpels, and trays in seed banks.
I feel I've wasted the gift of good seed.

I do not yet know that regardless of my care and attention, I will not see any of these plants to their fruiting stage.
That I will not save their seeds, because I will move back
across borders by the time the tomatoes blush from green,
before all the flowers on the chillies have formed crooked,
glossy fruit. That I will gift them all, in a strange act of
circularity, to Nina in the weeks before I go.

"Optimism is pathological ignorance of the facts." I
cannot remember where I encountered this phrase; perhaps
I read this once on a meme, or a bumper sticker, or maybe
heard it in a self-help group or a TED talk. I've probably
given it too much thought in the years since. I do not think
of myself as an optimist, though friends tell me that they

think I am. I worry, most days, about the future: nagging fears about job security, and making rent, and whether our world will cease to become habitable at all. That it already has. But still I want to grow things.

What would it be to stay in a place long enough to save its seeds? I do not yet know the answer, but I hope I might. I do know that when I planted these seeds, I was forty weeks pregnant. Surely I believe in some kind of future?

In her meditation on creating a garden to attract monarch butterflies in her Toronto backyard, the environmental humanities scholar Cate Sandilands asks about the nature of hope, and whether hope in our moment is misplaced. I think of these questions from time to time, when I buy seeds, or when I plan the next season's garden, or think of creating a beauty that cannot last. Would time better be spent agitating for societal change? What use is a single garden—or indeed, in my case, a single seed? Saving seeds is an act of belief in a future that the present tells me cannot exist, but I do it anyway.

Two things can be true at once.

13.

Pinetum

I. *PINUS MUNDAYI*

In 2011, a team of researchers uncovered a series of fossils at the Bailey Quarry near Windsor, Nova Scotia. The remnants of charred twigs were no larger than two centimetres long and surrounded with gypsum. Howard Falcon-Lang, the lead researcher, boxed them up and sent them back to London. They remained in a drawer untouched for years.

In 2016, these twigs took up headlines. The area they had been found in was known for deposits dating back to the Cretaceous Period, between 66 and 145 million years ago. Falcon-Lang had finally dissolved their surrounding gypsum in hydrofluoric acid and rinsed them with distilled water, releasing tiny pieces of charcoal. The pieces were examined with a scanning electron microscope and then dissected with a scalpel and examined once again. Each showed the suggestive characteristics of a pine tree: tubular resin ducts surrounded by thin-walled epithelial cells, and the bases for fascicles of two needles. Based on these characteristics, Falcon-Lang determined his twigs to be of an unnamed species, an early example from an age before our present pines came into existence. He offered *Pinus mundayi* as their Latin binomial, in honour of two Welsh physicians—Derek and Mary Munday—who had guided him through treatment for Lyme disease he'd contracted during his fieldwork. The fossils, at 133 to 140 million years old, are the oldest known examples of a pine tree in history.

For a long time, it was difficult to accurately classify pines. They have large genomes, and many species have chromosomes that look rather alike. But there are some things we know with certainty.

Pines—the genus *Pinus* specifically—emerged around 150 million years ago, dispersed across the Northern Hemisphere before North America, Europe, and Asia broke apart. Oaks did not yet exist, nor beeches, nor birches. The world then was warmer, and pines specialised early in surviving difficult conditions, eventually finding a home extending from north of the Arctic Circle as far south as the tropics. Such a range could be possible only through adaptation: some tended towards low-nutrient soils and extremely cold or hot temperatures, while others adapted for fire.

The pines, you might then say, are venturing trees. Tenacious, innovative, adaptable. Their pollen and seeds spread exceptionally well by wind. And they are incredibly useful for humans, who have aided in their spread around the globe. For all these reasons pines are also especially helpful for understanding invasions.

There is a tendency to group many trees under the title "pine." A pinetum is simply a collection of conifers and might well include cypresses, cedars, firs, yews, and larches amidst the pines. Because botanically, conifers are officially known as the Pinophyta, with all existing species belonging to the order Pinales. Pines—of which there are more than a hundred species—stand in, as shorthand, for many more trees than themselves.

But there is another taxonomy by which I understand the pine.

II. *PINUS STROBUS*

Pine Ridge was a suburb inside a suburb, a more affluent stretch of houses arranged in a U shape around a stand of eastern white pine trees. Before Pine Ridge was built, the forest bordered on farmland and houses, all of which would soon be bought up to build a few strip malls and one very large shopping mall. This was 1988. Winter left snow on the verge of our new road, right up to the communal mailbox that sat at the end of our new driveway. Everything smelled cold and new and faintly of fresh timber.

The plot my parents bought extended a hundred feet into the trees, so that we had not just a large patch of grass in our backyard but our very own forest. At least, to a child, it felt vast. All the houses on our side of the street backed onto these trees, and because the houses were new, no one had fences put in yet. The forest became the territory of the neighbourhood kids. We'd meet in the middle, where no one knew whose backyard they were in anymore, and gather sticks for building forts. All the trees were identical, lanky pines already grown tall, so there was little to be climbed beyond the nubs left by branches hacked away. We'd cut across the darkness of trees to another family's backyard, where there was a treehouse, a swing, and a set of monkey bars off of which every local child would one day tumble. We'd spend entire weekend days in this forest, making believe, warning one another of suburban legends and which neighbourhood houses to avoid on Halloween (always, everyone agreed, the one on the corner where no kids lived). Each winter I collected the stray pinecones that dotted the snow in our yard, clustering them in a basket indoors, their clear scent clinging to my fingers. Our city called itself the Forest City—and here, as a child, it felt true. The forest gave us shelter to run wild—to play, experiment, and imagine—though we didn't fully understand it at the time.

We played until the parents decided to put in fences, stretches of wood or coils of wire that reached out into our woodland, blocking it off into tidy squares. It was safer then, the parents all said, because strangers couldn't wander into one another's backyards. It had been a few years, and all the families who'd moved into the area with young kids were suddenly grappling with teenagers. Then the forest began to signify danger. We didn't tell them that the teens all gathered in an opening in the corn field at the end of the lane, where they'd light bonfires and roll joints. That a patch of trees from which we could still see home wasn't exactly illicit. I can't say what other ideas were projected onto those trees, but I do know that once there was a fence, I stopped wandering into them entirely. What was the point if I couldn't go anywhere at all? And besides, half the pines in the neighbourhood were sick and needed to be felled. The houses had been built too close to their roots, an arborist told us. On our plot alone, nine pines withered and gave way to grass.

III. *PINUS SYLVESTRIS*

I did not think seriously about forests until I was a teenager, and then only at the bidding of my schoolteachers. We read *A Midsummer Night's Dream* and *Macbeth* and analysed the way setting shaped a story's possibilities, the way tree canopies gave shelter to mischief, and the way the slow succession of forests signified a tightening circle of fate. We talked about fairy tales—Little Red Riding Hood and Hansel and Gretel—and I thought often of the forest behind our house. But after I left home, I lived for years in places where I rarely saw pines at all.

Then, in 2014, I moved to Germany, where it seemed

that so many of the cultural ideas I had about forests had originated. This was the east, and very little ancient woodland remained. But there were pines: an infinitude of Scots pines laid over a flat landscape. It was winter the first time I walked the forest path north of Liepnitzsee. There, where the beech and oak forest ended, a tangled stand of pine grew. Its branches hadn't been cut back, giving the impression not of a woodland one could enter, but of a forbidden forest: thorny, dark, green dulled by the mist that hung low to the ground. Here, I thought, was the pine of the Brothers Grimm, the kind of forest where I'd find Baba Yaga. I was reminded of a painting I'd seen reprinted in a book: Caspar David Friedrich's *Der Chasseur im Wald* from 1814, painted during the French occupation of Germany, just two years after the Grimms first published their collection of stories. In the image, a lone French soldier encounters a wall of trees. But the trees are not impenetrable—rather, the only forward path in the painting is into its darkness.

Of course, in reality the trees I encountered held little of these stories. This was a working landscape, and almost all the pine trees in the land around Berlin belonged to managed plantations. Every so often a stand would be marked out with spray paint, hemmed in with barricade tape. The next time I returned, tidy stacks of logs stood at the perimeter where the trees once were.

In her study of fairy tales and forests, Sara Maitland writes that the forests of northern Europe are precisely the landscape out of which European folktales could grow; that the very content of stories built on getting lost, or finding some promised but hidden reward, or thwarting deception all relied upon a kind of environment in which the very same possibilities held true. Forest trails wind and enclose around you. Dangerous fungi are disguised as delectable. In forests—as opposed to deserts, she writes—we can therefore tell different kinds of stories than we can elsewhere. This deep relationship between place and cultural production meant that in Germany, around the time the Brothers Grimm were working, forests became linked to a Romantic—and later nationalist—self-image. A century on, the forests would hold very different legacies: One pinewood I walked south of the capital was still turning up remains of soldiers and civilians from the Second World War. In another, at the end of a plantation I found a dilapidated nineteenth-century castle fit for a fairy tale. It had been requisitioned by Himmler, and its grounds had been renovated by the prisoners of a nearby concentration camp.

Over the years in this place, I often walked in the forests alone. Each time, I felt a little bit afraid. It was the stories I'd read and the idea of being a woman alone in the woods. Most of the trails cut through the trees in straight lines, only occasionally bisected by angled paths that left me disoriented. Often, I had no phone signal, so I attuned my senses to the environment around me: the glint of sunlight between high branches, the smell that emanated from the sand underfoot whenever I approached water. I focussed on the colours of each tree I saw—burnt-orange bark and deep-green foliage—asking how something so brightly hued could exist in winter. I recited the names of forest species, learning each of their shapes across the seasons. Scots pine, heather, bilberry. Rugose fork moss, glittering wood moss. Eventually my skin stopped prickling at every dark thought, and my head stopped turning at every creak from the timber above.

Scots pine is the most widely distributed pine in the world, with a natural range that stretches from Eastern Siberia to Spain, Scandinavia to the Sierra Nevada. The tree does well in soils poor in nutrients and prone to disturbance—which is just as well, as it is mostly planted to be felled again. But it is humans that have expanded its range: having been planted in North America as a commercial species, very often for Christmas trees, it is now described there as invasive. I read descriptions of the species written from this other lens—so far from the sylvan stories of the land in which they belong—and find a militarised language. The Scots pine, I learn, is a hardy coloniser. It is known to escape cultivation. It will naturalise in a habitat to which it cannot belong.

IV. *PINUS NIGRA*

I have begun to collect pines in my life. I do not realise it at first, but I am noting their subtle differences—the shape of a cone, the thickness of bark, the way a spray of needles drapes from a branch.

One morning, during the year we live in Cambridge, we get up early to drive to Thetford. It is July, and I am expecting to smell the forest before I see the trees up close. Here the pines grow thick where they've not yet been felled. Douglas firs crowd the trail, and small oak seedlings are reaching for the summer light. I am searching, perhaps, for a scent I've known in other forests: citrus and green, something clean on the air. I am searching for a black pine.

In 1785, after a journey around Mariazell in the Austrian Alps, the German botanist Johann Franz Xaver Arnold described a resinous pine tree unlike any he had encountered before. In the final pages of his *Reise nach Mariazell in Steyermark* he included an etching of the species, with long needles in fascicles of two and tight oval cones. He named it *Pinus nigra*, the black pine, a tree perhaps now best known for two subspecies: the Austrian black pine Arnold encountered and the Corsican black pine (*Pinus nigra* subsp. *laricio*) more commonly found around the Mediterranean.

While the Austrian subspecies did not reach Britain until roughly 1835, the Corsican pine had been introduced as early as 1759. It is now the dominant black pine in the United Kingdom, largely due to its value as a timber tree. Quick growing, its straight, tall form lends itself to the uses of industry: as railway sleepers, telephone poles, roofing, flooring, pallets, and pulp. It thrives where most species will not—in sandy soil, on sea-blasted outcrops, and on parched ground. So following the loss of huge swathes of Britain's forests during the First World War, it was at Thetford in 1922 that Corsican black pines were originally chosen to create a new forest.

The ground in the Breckland of East Anglia is thin and sandy, thus deemed suitable for the creation of a forest en masse. Pines would grow quickly here, particularly the Corsicans. So when by 1924, some two thousand of the eleven thousand acres of land acquired had already been planted out, it was to the Forestry Commission chairman's surprise that the bulk of these early plantings were of native Scots pine. The motivation for this swap, the chairman later wrote, was due to a fear of frost-tenderness and a "prejudice against Corsican timber (in which prominent timber merchants shared)." But when infestations of pine shoot moths decimated stands of Scots pine, Corsican became the tree of choice as a matter of policy. Huge swathes of land were planted with the species, such that from the 1930s until 2006, when a moratorium on the planting of Corsican pine came into effect due to its vulnerability to *Dothistroma* needle blight, the Thetford Forest—England's largest lowland pine forest—became synonymous with *Pinus nigra*.

Some years before Thetford, I spent a few weeks identifying herbarium specimens at Kew. The course centred on angiosperms—plants that flower and fruit—rather than conifers and mosses, which interest me more. At lunchtime, I often walked out into the gardens, hoping to see as much as I could with the visitor's pass the course granted me. But the pinetum was at the opposite end of the property and I could only ever make it as far as the rhododendrons before having to turn back to get to lessons again. Near the herbarium, though, I found a single pine tree: an Austrian black pine in a mulched-over bed along a pathway in the back. It was remarkably straight, with metallic scales climbing its trunk, and a bushy, dark spray of branches near its top. Standing beneath it, I could think only of the backyard pines I grew up with.

The next summer, I added to my collection while visiting my family. Cones, needles, small clusters of evergreen life that I found dotted around the ground of the cottage, a place where jack pines and white pines reach out across the rocks. I arranged them along the windowsill and began the work of identifying the trees by their cones and small clusters of needles. I did not look at the trunks from which they'd fallen—I wanted to learn the skill of identification in abstraction. In pines, needles usually cluster in fascicles of two, three, or five. Only one of the trees was a pine: the white pine I knew well, notable for its groupings of five needles and long cones. The rest I labelled with care: a tiny cone from an eastern hemlock, a sturdy snippet of yew, a soft bauble of balsam fir. I filed their forms away in my mind, recorded the feel of their needles, cones, and bark.

What I had in mind was a pinetum: an imagined one, perhaps, a place to hold all the pines I had ever known. Where pines that spanned vast distances would feel, to me, like home.

V. *PINUS TAIWANENSIS*

But beyond my imagination, pinetums prove surprisingly plentiful, and in them I find the vastness of the world condensed. I browse the trees at Bedgebury National Pinetum in the southeast of England—considered the world's most complete collection of conifers—searching for cedars and cypresses I've seen only in Taiwan. In Cambridge, at the Botanic Gardens, in a clearing called the Old Pinetum, I come upon a small patch where pines far from their native ranges grow together: Scots pine, Austrian pine, American pinyon, and Chinese white pine. I stand there in the middle of the world, sunlight reaching at soft angles through the spray of green.

In spring one year, my husband takes me to Chatsworth. We buy passes to the gardens but immediately wander to the far edge of the grounds, where the map tells us we will find a pinetum. We follow a path through dappled shade and light, sheltered on one side by a hill, until we cannot carry on. The trees grow larger and less carefully tended the farther we walk: Japanese white pine and Douglas fir, giant redwood and cedar of Lebanon. Juniper and larch, its needles dangling towards the soft grass. I try to name the trees aloud, and my husband takes careful photographs of each branch as we pass. There, in the middle of England, where chestnut woodland presses hard against the museum-piece of an estate garden, I show him my childhood tree, the eastern white pine.

Of course, a pinetum is a shadow of a pine forest. It serves only to remind us of what has lived—and what might cease to live—in vast swathes of our world. There are pines I may never get to see. It seems silly to write that—of course, there are many species I will never encounter, and many disappearing all the time—but the more I read of the genus, the more I want to collect as many as I can.

In studies of biodiversity, scientists refer to something called a latitudinal diversity gradient, whereby more species diversity is concentrated towards the equator, gradually thinning out towards the poles. Imagine the glut of a tropical forest compared to the sparseness of cold tundra. Conifers, curiously, do not follow this gradient. Rather, their diversity is crowded in the middle latitudes of the Northern Hemisphere: a map of pine distribution shows a band that winds around our globe, never straying too far south. On the map, I pause over an area of intense concentration: in Mexico, there are more pine species than anywhere else on our planet, most of which are much younger than the old-world pine species we know in Europe and Asia. Researchers believe these species to be southward migrants from both east and west of the region, diversified in response to the dramatic cooling of the climate nearly thirty-four million years ago. That so much diversity exists despite their curious distribution is a matter of their chosen topography—and to mountains, with their rapid shifts in elevation and temperature, especially.

It was on a mountain in Central Taiwan that I began to think of pines not as relics of my own and this planet's deep past, but as portals to its future. The trail on which I stood was narrow, a hard-packed line of gravel bordered on one side by a steep drop towards the valley below. A landslide had cut away a swathe of rock hundreds of metres across, leaving a greying wound in the mountainside. But amidst the scree grew tiny tufts of green life, islands in stone. The Taiwanese red pine—*Pinus taiwanensis*—is a striking tree, with erect branches mirroring the peaks on which it grows. On slopes denuded by earthquakes, typhoons, and landslides, it is a vital pioneer of devastated ground. Where landslides carry all life away, grasses begin the process of succession. And then the roots of Taiwanese red pine work to restore integrity to the mountainside.

It is this idea of pine that I return to: pines as trees of resurrection, as migrants making do, as species that restore forests after fires. Researchers know from phylogenetic studies that pines diversified early in their history and have repeatedly diversified again: 90 percent of the pines that exist today originated in the Miocene, between five and twenty million years ago, in response to dramatic climatic shifts. Over their lifetimes, they have adapted to a world more prone to fire, to a drier world, to heat, to cold. I think of *Pinus mundayi*, the oldest pine. And all the others that are yet to come.

14.

Synonyms for "Mauve"

mauve (*n. or adj.*) There was a time when I learned to see beauty. It was not the only beauty I would ever know, but it was the first and it was the most intoxicating. This, I need to explain.

I cannot account for the future of this world, or why I brought you into it, other than to say that I believe beauty is worthwhile. I know that you will not live the same kind of life that I did. You will grow up in another country, with other kinds of joys. Perhaps I only want to make a record. Not that I would ever forget the feeling it gave me: that feeling returns every time I see a purple flower, an English garden, an open heath. But you are new in this world, to colour and to light. If I explain, perhaps, you might see it, too. Or you may know why we are here, and not there, or another place altogether.

I am six, and it is the first time my parents have taken me back to Britain. School is on back home, and I am missing three weeks of grade one for this visit. I am cataloguing the things I see and do so that I can share them in show-and-tell. So far I've hung laundry on a line in the garden with Auntie Joan and Uncle Ronnie. This I love. We aren't allowed to hang things outside back home, so I've never seen a laundry line before. The garden is bordered with spring onions and lavender. We've taken a train up a Welsh mountain into white fog. I've gone to school for a day with my cousin Gareth and felt silly because I have no school uniform and do not speak Welsh (of course, it was Welsh class that day).

I have travelled a lot in my life already, but I have never been to a place that feels homelike. Never to a place with so much family, or laundry pegs, or brown vinegar on chips. Everything I see feels, somehow, like something I already know.

Before the trip, I can list the things I know about Britain, absorbed osmotically each afternoon that I spend with my grandparents.

I wish you could have known them, because they gave me so much.

Nanny and Bampi moved from Cardiff to Canada to help my parents after my older sister was born. Every day before I start full-day school, Bamp uses his lunch break from work to pick me up from nursery or kindergarten, then drives us home for lunch (which he calls dinner) cooked earlier that day by Nan. Every day, I put on the same brown gingham pinny that Nan sewed for me. We eat mashed potatoes and gravy and boiled vegetables with roast pork, or sliced chicken, or sometimes corned beef hash pie or fried rissoles. We have cups of tea and digestives bought from Marks & Spencer, and watch Thomas the Tank Engine on the little TV in the corner.

Sometimes if Bamp is in a foul mood, he tells us it is a "Blitzkrieg" day and gets me to polish the figurines by the fireplace with a can of Brasso. (This is where I learn the word "Blitzkrieg"—it will be a long time before I learn it has any other meaning.)

Once Bamp goes back to work, Nan and I read, paint, and play all afternoon. While Bampi normally paints oils in the style of Bob Ross, Nanny leans across the polished wood dining table and teaches me to create watercolour landscapes like hers: purple fields and tousled cottage gardens. We do paint-by-numbers that she has brought from Britain and paint pictures from old photographs of gardens and calendars of Welsh castles. Picture after picture of Castell Coch. And she shows me, petal by petal, how to press my brush to paper, how to make arcs that look leaflike and alive. With Nan and a set of paints, I come to know what British plants are: hollyhocks, hawthorn, gooseberries, and gorse.

Nan and Bamp give me picture books they've bought on trips back home. Beatrix Potter stories with farmers' fields, Roald Dahl anthologies, and a handful of books about badgers. They're on your shelf now—you'll see my name scrawled in pencil on the first page of each. I read them all. But more often I just gaze at the pictures, the scenery behind the woodland creatures wearing clothes. These are places that look nothing like where I live. I've never seen a badger, or a hedgehog, or a hare. In our backyard, the wildest thing I know is a stand of pines.

The nature Nan shows me has a colour so unlike the browns of those trees. In my favourite books, the ground is an etched tangle of growth. There are saturated greens, glowing pinks, hazy blues. All is mist and softness. Nan teaches me colours that are the names of flowers: iris, lilac, lavender. A purple I love but have trouble describing. Nanny tells me it is called mauve. This is a word I've never heard used by anyone else. A word I feel unsure of how and when to use. But I decide then that it is my favourite.

I think many children choose purple as their favourite colour. I do not now think my love of purple was special.

But I called purple "mauve." (So maybe I did think it was
special.)

"Mauve" comes from the Latin word "malva" and the
French word for the mallow flower. If I want to tell you the
colour of a mallow flower, I need another word for "mauve."

But the Oxford thesaurus I've carried for a decade skips
from "mausoleum" to "maverick."

"Sorry, no results for 'mauve' in the Collins English
Thesaurus."

Thesaurus.com lists five synonyms for "mauve." The
fifth—"violaceous"—sounds absurd, so I click on it first.
The entry says only "as in mauve" and "as in purple." And
lists the same other synonyms—"lavender," "lilac," "plum,"
"violet." These relations don't tell me anything about colour.

Instead, I will try to explain.

On that visit to Britain, we've been throughout Wales, to
London, and to Cornwall. It is the end of the trip, and
we are in Devon, where one of my uncles lives. We are on

horseback, on a tourist trek across Dartmoor, and no one seems very happy. It is October, so the air is cold. It will not stop raining. My dad and sister have pulled their raincoats tight around them. My cousins are crying because they are afraid of ponies. Muck squelches around the ponies' hooves, sticks in clumps to their dappled legs. But I feel a pulsing in my chest, a breath catching in my throat. There is a slate sky smudged into uneven ground, and a floral carpet glowing into the distance. For the first time, I am in a landscape I've seen before, but only ever in books and paintings. I am in the exact softness Nan taught me. And all around me, there is heather.

I try to find words for what I see. And the only word I can find is "mauve."

heather (*n. or adj.*) *Calluna vulgaris*, commonly called heather or ling, is a shrub that thrives on acidic, free-draining soil—on heathlands and moors across the north of Europe. On landscapes swathed in colour. In winter and spring, the related *Erica* genus of heaths bloom, and in summer and autumn heather itself comes into flower. The species thrives in a delicate balance: If overgrazed, it dies back. If the growth of young trees is not abated, it gives way to forest. Needing careful maintenance, heather's habitats are anthropogenic places, long kept in stasis through the measured use of fire. In turn, heather provides fodder for livestock and grouse, as well as other bird species who shelter in its low growth. In beauty, it provides a value that is more difficult to quantify.

Before that day on Dartmoor, I have never seen heather. It isn't a plant that grows wild in southern Ontario, and it isn't common amongst the tidied lawns and ornamental gardens where we live. Growing up, I'll come to know heather instead through the lens of literature we are assigned in high school: In *Jane Eyre*, where on the moor Jane finds herself sleeping nights upon the heath, "wild and unproductive," only to wake to the landscape's beauty illuminated by sunlight. In grade eleven we will read *Wuthering Heights*, where Cathy longs to be free and wild upon the land: "I'm sure I should be myself were I once among the heather of these hills." In the Brontës' books, women roam sublime, stony landscapes that are carved out by cold winds. Heather is everpresent. As a teenager I'll carry these novels with me and wonder what it might mean to be a woman in a wild land.

I do not need to understand the workings of empire for it to shape me profoundly; though it is never framed in critical terms, the idea of being from a colony at arm's length from the centre pervades school life. In history lessons, we work from a book illustrated with brown etchings, showing the ways British and French settlers carved territory in the image of their homelands: patchwork fields for the British land, narrow bands for the French. We learn that Canadian land was once seen as waste to be domesticated, not beautiful in itself. Which is to say: not like the land from which colonists came. Not like the land my family was from.

Simply through repetition—in storybooks and novels deemed classics, curricula—British landscapes come to signify romance, an ideal in nature. I pay no attention to flora outside my window—in a flat land of canola and corn, where forests are built of sugar maples and pines. I read so little of these plants, and in truth, they hold little interest for me. It will take me years before I realise that I've built my notions of beauty from the stories of a distant land.

lavender (*n. or adj.*) I am eighteen and leaving home, moving my life to the coast for university. I like the idea of Nova Scotia, of living by the sea. I've boxed up photographs of school friends and boyfriends, packed books and clothes for the year. I have posters from English bands I've been listening to on a livestream from a London radio station. I've left hardly anything of value behind. I have no intention of ever returning to my hometown again.

Nova Scotia is like nowhere I've been before, but it is like something from my imagination: stony beaches and grey water. Fog so thick that the boat bells ring loud even miles from the harbour. I take to walking against the wind, along the docks, around the peninsula, a raincoat tight against me, breathing rain and tasting salt. The ground I watch is rocky, grey, and studded with lupins. Every colour in fog feels desaturated, plums turned to greys. Lavender grows in great bunches outside the building where I live. I find beauty in it all. But though I can't explain why, I am still fixated on the idea of elsewhere. Standing at the tip of Point Pleasant Park, I imagine drawing an angled line to Britain, thousands of miles across the sea. To the landscapes I've been taught. That confrontation with beauty.

What I want is to see heather.

In L. M. Montgomery's novel *Anne of the Island*, the third book in the Anne of Green Gables series, Anne is studying in Nova Scotia. The places she visits are loosely fictionalised, but I can lay them like tracing paper atop places I know. In one scene, Anne and her friends visit a place analogous to Point Pleasant Park. Anne is rapturous at the beauty of it, and the conversation turns to how such places remind the group of books.

(Have I, at times, been as rapturous as Anne?)

"Speaking of romance," said Priscilla, *"we've been looking for heather—but, of course, we couldn't find any. It's too late in the season, I suppose."*

"Heather!" exclaimed Anne. *"Heather doesn't grow in America, does it?"*

"There are just two patches of it in the whole continent," said Phil, *"one right here in the park, and one somewhere else in Nova Scotia, I forget where. The famous Highland Regiment, the Black Watch, camped here one year, and, when the men shook out the straw of their beds in the spring, some seeds of heather took root."*

When I begin to search, I learn that heather had been documented on the continent for many decades before L. M. Montgomery wrote *Anne of the Island.* Throughout the nineteenth century, shrubs of it were found in Massachusetts, Newfoundland, and elsewhere in Nova Scotia. Within a hundred years, twenty-nine sightings were recorded. One sighting stands out: in 1861 it was submitted to a Massachusetts horticultural show as "native" heather, a claim that caused so much controversy entire botanical teams were sent to investigate it. At first it was thought that those who'd collected the plant had been mistaken. But the botanists could identify *Calluna vulgaris* by its leaves arranged at right angles along the stem, by its late-summer flowers along a single shoot. They knew what it was and argued over whether it should be classed as "native" or "introduced." Since it was only ever found in dwindling patches, some supposed perhaps the plant *was* native to North America but likely facing extinction on the continent.

In 1876, a botanist named George Lawson tried to explain. The patch in Point Pleasant, he observed, looked intentionally planted, free of other plants and debris, on a bed cleared from rocky ground. He made enquiries of specimens found in Newfoundland, only to be told that they had been brought as bedding plants for the garden of Lord Baltimore two hundred years before. But on receiving reports of heather growing around Nova Scotia in seemingly wild and uncultivated places, of such quantity as to become established (for heather is a slow-growing plant), Lawson still reached the conclusion shared by his contemporaries that the plants *must* be native to North America. That the desire to attribute its presence to the Highland Regiment was simply tied to an idea that the plant *must* be foreign, because of all it signified. Lawson saw a desire to link heather to colonial origin stories, to tales of past homelands. To heather as romance.

Lawson's account is not alone. There are many reports on heather from the time, all with titles that raise the question of belonging: "American heather" and "The heather (*Calluna vulgaris*), a native of the United States."

In a 1958 round-up of heather research from the previous decades, botanist Roy B. Clarkson writes that heather "received more attention . . . than any other plant of comparable distribution in America." Why should a scrubby, slow-growing plant documented in so few places draw such excitement?

The consensus today is that *Calluna vulgaris* was in fact introduced to North America, but in such quantities that it now grows seemingly wild in the few places it may be found. It is a plant with multiple origin stories. A plant naturalised on colonised land.

In *Anne of the Island*, Montgomery repeats a traditional tale, recounted in the scientific literature of the period, almost verbatim: it was brought by Highland soldiers in their bedding or their brooms. Her characters take up the spirit of the botanical—and colonial—question: Could this plant belong in this place? And, likewise, could the beauty it signifies belong here, too? In four years, I never see heather growing in Nova Scotia. But in Anne, Montgomery reveals an emotional taxonomy by which I understand it: as worthy of fascination. As romantic, joyful, and deeply longed-for.

bramble (*n. or adj.*) In her essay "Small Bodies of Water," Nina Mingya Powles writes of moving to England after a childhood in New Zealand: "I learn the names of trees that have featured in the pictures of stories I've read since childhood but never seen in real life. The words sound almost mythical to me now: alder, hazel, yew, ash."

At twenty-one, I am moving at last to Britain. I have an offer for a master's programme in London to study landscape aesthetics. I have in mind a life of walking and writing in places I've long idealised.

(I am moving in search of beauty.)

The flat is in Dartmouth Park, stamped out of the first floor of a Victorian terrace the landlords have inherited. All the walls are at strange angles. The kitchen window is missing a pane of glass, but wanting to make the best of it, I tell myself I'm lucky to have found the flat. I seal the gap with cardboard and packing tape. From that window I have a view of the garden below, and beyond it, the sky over Hampstead Heath. This is a place I have heard of but never seen up close. A place already formed in my imagination.

To me the Heath is Hugh Grant walking through an ivy tunnel in *Notting Hill*. It is Zadie Smith novels, and edgeland walks by Richard Mabey. By its name I expect a rugged land. But what I find instead are rolling fields, overgrown hedgerows, and shaded woodland paths. Hills that slope at just the right angles to catch the late-day light. A view of church spires and red shingled roofs. A glimpse of the city beyond. This place is so perfect it seems drawn from the pictures Nan and I painted. It does not look like the heathland I remember. But I cannot deny it has its own kind of beauty.

That spring I see for the first time a hedgerow in white bloom. I put a name to it: "hawthorn," a word I've turned over in my mouth so many times before. Common hawthorn grows plentifully in Canada, having been introduced by British settlers, but until I see it in Britain, I don't know how to recognise it. I learn the buttercream blooms and flat green leaves, shaped like a piece of parsley. From there, I begin to learn what grows here. Young leaves of red sorrel, sour on my tongue. Berries in the brambles in late summer. A deep purple saturates my skin. All these are plants that grow weedy where I come from; but here, I feel I can somehow know them better. That this is a place in which they belong.

My grandparents may have come from Wales, but I can't shake the feeling they would have loved this English landscape. Was this the sort of nature they tried to paint themselves back towards?

My father does not like it when I speak of England. But after forty years in Canada, he no longer sounds very Welsh.

I spend my master's thinking about beauty and our aesthetic experiences of belonging. I title my dissertation "HOME LIFE." Because I cannot stop thinking about how we make our lives work, what it feels like to be at home. I do not write that I imagine home to be the colour mauve, though I do.

When I am finished, this question of beauty holds fast. So I turn to a doctorate thinking about the Heath, because I want to understand why, before I came here, I felt I already knew this place. Before ever having seen it. Why some landscapes are written into the record in ways that others are not. How we imagine and make for ourselves a perfect, idealised nature.

I write that when we speak of conservation, it is essential to ask exactly which vision of a place we are conserving. Which means doing history.

The summer of 2012 falls a year into my doctoral work. This is a summer when "Bread of Heaven" and "Jerusalem" are sung in a medley by children, when England's green and pleasant land is worn as a badge of honour. For a time, it becomes fashionable to love this place as naively as I do.

Of course, it isn't the land that is the problem. Land wears human guises—and these cannot easily be stripped away.

Raymond Williams, my favourite cultural critic on nature, writes that "the self-regarding patriotism of the high English imperialist period found this sweetest and most insidious of its forms in a version of the rural past." Is this the beauty I am writing of?

I don't yet know how to admit that the reason I need to ask these questions is so deeply personal; that I need to know why this vision of beauty feels so salient to me. I know it is in part because it signifies familial love. But I suppose I am admitting to a kind of privilege here; it is only in writing this thesis that I will begin to see that I've been shaped within the ideological reach of empire.

In his 1629 *Iter Plantarum* and 1632 *Descriptio Itineris*, Thomas Johnson records a modest array of plants over two visits to Hampstead Heath. After Gerard's *Herball*, which took in far more than just the Heath, Johnson's are the earliest floras of the site. His Heath is true to its name: an open landscape of acidic soil, Eocene sand deposits, and heathland plants. Common heather, bell heather, gorse, bilberry, and juniper. An anthropogenic habitat held as common land—for grazing livestock, harvesting shrubs and wood. A place that needs use, burning, and scrub clearance if the trees are to be held at bay.

In the eighteenth century, and the nineteenth, too, the Heath held a similar sort of fascination to my own. People came: for therapeutic waters at Hampstead, for fresh air on the Heath. For fairground rapture on bank holiday weekends—they came in their hundreds of thousands. As London came for the Heath, digging came, too. The land was taken to build a city around it.

In his account of the damage wrought by sand and gravel extraction on the Heath, the chairman of the Commons Preservation Society Lord Eversley specifically mourns the loss of heather. Sand extraction was damaging "to the extent of destroying its herbage and heather." Digging, he writes, was being "carried out to a degree that threatened to interfere with the natural features of Hampstead Heath" and "the Heath was most seriously injured."

I spend entire afternoons walking chasms left where sand was once dug. Trees have encroached there now. But two hundred years on from digging, the depth of this damage still remains.

In 1913, Arthur George Tansley, a botanist with the Hampstead Scientific Society, observed that the Heath had been converted entirely to grass-heathland. It was no longer, to use his term, a "true heath."

Which Heath, I ask, is the truest?

I spend five years writing of this place, until I have sucked its beauty clean from bone. Not once do I see heather grow wild on these hills. Instead, as if to sate my longing, I have its shape tattooed on my skin. A single branch, cut close to the ribs.

Tyrian purple (*n. or adj.*) Nan always told me that purple was a royal colour. A colour prized because of how difficult it was, in previous centuries, to render as dye by boiling marine molluscs for ten days in brine. On a map of ancient Mediterranean "purple-producing sites," the seacoast is littered with purple dots. These purple places—uncovered by researchers using spectrometry and chromatography and ancient literature—are so entwined with the history of the colour that encyclopaedia entries on "purple" will tell you not about the colour in its wild form, but about how costly it was for ancient civilisations to produce it.

In one book I read, the colour purple is a gift from God. But purple is also a bruise.

It isn't until 1856 that a man—one William Henry Perkin—synthesises purple. He does it by accident: As

Britain is extending its empire across the Southern Hemisphere, quinine becomes an essential substance in the battle against malaria. Perkin is trying to synthesise quinine the day he makes a dye he calls Tyrian purple. One of its other names is imperial purple.

I read in the newspaper that Perkins later renamed this colour "mauve."

Three years on from finishing my work on the Heath, I spend my days writing. As if to make up for the years I idealised it, I've stopped writing about Britain. I've moved to Germany, and in that time 51 percent of British voters have voted to leave the European Union.

I am learning to cleave my memory of my grandparents and the beauty they loved from the place of its becoming. Britishness is not a comfortable, cosy thing right now. But this is not news to anyone who has known the meaning of empire.

I cannot tell you where beauty is in a hostile environment.

In these years I seek heather in other places: in forests in the east of Germany, on ground that is anything but neutral to those who know it. This is a land on which I can place no expectations. Its history is not mine; its beauty more complicated. Still, I learn to love it. I make a home, get married.

In a winter month, I am invited to read on a nature writing panel in Yorkshire. I have never been to Yorkshire. So I fly to Manchester, take a train into the Calder Valley, and climb to a hilltop reservoir to swim. I gather with a group of writers in the upstairs room of a pub and I read for an audience from a book about my mother's notion of beauty: about landscape in Taiwan, about her parents. I do not talk about Britain, about heather, or about mauve. The others read about whale falls and eels that travel an entire ocean to make a life elsewhere.

After the panel finishes, I speak with one of the other authors, a poet named Zaffar Kunial. He tells me he is the poet-in-residence at Haworth, at the Brontë Parsonage Museum, and invites me to visit the museum with him the next morning.

I do not say out loud what visiting this place means to me.

At eight forty-five, we board the Brontë Bus, which ferries tourists and locals across the moors between Hebden Bridge and Keighley. The bus moves so swiftly that the hills outside the windows blur. Rain streaks across the panes. Ramblers in waterproofs climb on and off at stops along the Pennine

Way. Zaffar and I talk over the noise of it, and though we've only just met, I feel comfortable admitting that I've felt stuck in my writing. We name the plants that weave throughout our work: Zaffar tells me about a laburnum tree in his childhood garden. And I tell him of my love for heather. I have never told anyone about this. I tell him that I want this love to be neutral and easy. But it's bound up with my questions about beauty, how England takes up space in the cultural imagination even if you aren't from here.

Underneath, I know the discomfort our conversation points towards: words like "migrant," like "colony." At the crest of the hills, the bus jolts to a stop and we disembark.

Haworth is built of greying stone—quarried from local valleys—with a cluster of cottages set along a steep hill. At the top sits the parsonage where the Brontës once lived and wrote. Zaffar takes me into the museum's archive, where he's called ahead. The staff bring out rarely seen letters from Anne and Branwell and books that had belonged to each of the sisters. We look closely, leaning forward from cushioned seats as the staff hold them towards us. As a writer, I ought to be overjoyed; I am lucky to have this sort of access. But what I do not say is that I can't fully pay attention. I want most of all to be outside, in the wind and rain. The archive is warm and softly carpeted; the hillside better suits the place I've always imagined.

After, we wander into the fields where Emily once walked. A cold wind cuts over the heights, so I zip my jacket and wrap my scarf doubly around me. Zaffar wears his wool coat unbuttoned, as if immune to the weather. Frost on the grass crunches as I step to avoid puddles. We talk about the Brontës, of course, but mostly discuss his poetry, my books, wanting to write things and failing to. We talk about our hopes. At the end of our visit, he tells me he'll stay for the day to write, feeling inspired again. And I feel it, too. Something between longing for a place and a longing to write: I feel it now so rarely.

I ride the bus back to town alone, staring out the window. Dark stones and reds and oranges dot the slopes. The heather has turned to rust by now; it is too late in the season for purple. What would it mean to settle in this place? My worries about Britain still echo in my mind. But I ask myself then to look and keep looking. Is there not something here of vast beauty? I know that somehow the heather in these hills has shaped me, though I've never set foot here before.

red-violet (*n. or adj.*) The week you press yourself into my womb, heather brushes my ankles. We are in the Peak District. Your father and I spend our days walking, and in every place we go, I find myself thinking of that day in

Yorkshire. I want to say I am thinking of books, but really I am thinking of that scene in *Pride and Prejudice* (the Keira Knightley version). I find myself standing at Stanage Edge, even though I am afraid of heights. The dog is braver than me and inches towards the edge so that wind catches the fine hairs of his snout. We walk hills the entire week, slip into streams, and scramble a waterfall to reach the top of Kinder Scout. There are sunshine, rain, and snow together. We do not yet know you are with us already. We have only just moved back to Britain. But I think that if I am to raise a child here, this is how I want our life to be: all of us together, cold wetting our feet as we walk across a rugged land. Our world would be a mottled shade, the way I soon imagine yours might be, held in the darkness of my body.

The next week I am standing in the soft pink bathroom, and in my left hand is a white plastic stick. Outside, it is the middle of springtime; the world thrums with good-weather excitement, with joy at being allowed outdoors in groups. My phone is running a timer, and after a while it plays a chime too loud. After days of fretful curiosity, you are there: two red-violet lines, one slightly paler than the other.

lilac (*n. or adj.*) I can't remember how old I was when Nan unboxed a paint-by-numbers canvas for both of us to paint.

We'd often painted floral still-lifes—daffodils in vases, bouquets of lilacs and roses. But this painting promised something more. On the box, there was a cottage garden scene: a wooden bridge, a thatched roof, hollyhocks and lavender and daffodils lining a cobbled path. A pond lined with reeds and oak trees at the edges.

It looked exactly how I thought *home* ought to: everything compact and close, with nature pushing at the edges of indoor life. The most beautiful scene I'd ever known. We carefully rendered it in acrylics together, careful to match the colours to their numbers. I didn't think it kitsch at the time, didn't wonder how many identical paintings existed all around the world. We hung it in the bedroom at Nan's house, and then when she moved to a care home, we hung it above her bed. When I visited her and held her frail hand, shaking with Parkinson's, I wished us both into the scene: bright and at ease, surrounded by flowers. After she died, I inherited the painting.

In the years after, I looked at it often, trying to project myself into the garden scene as I had once done at her bedside. To imagine what that place might be like, where it might actually exist. No matter that it was prepared for us in a factory. I wanted to stand on the bridge, to walk towards the house. But I felt, too, an uneasiness in this longing. A sense that I was idealising something that wasn't entirely mine.

Now, I am six months pregnant with you and too tired to lift any boxes. The movers have deposited the largest items in their designated rooms, and I am making up for my unhelpfulness by planning: your cot can go here, the nursing chair by the window. I love this little box room, which looks out over the hawthorn tree and the lilacs and the footpath that runs behind our fence. I want to stand here in the window, to name every plant for you. The lilacs are a dusty shade of purple brown, faded with the summer heat. Like the outside of a passionfruit. Wisteria grows around the door, so the light in the entry has a periwinkle glow. We are new in Cambridge, still processing the notion of raising you here in England, but this little rented house by the river feels like a safe place for us to begin.

I've brought Nan's painting for you. My sister wrapped it in brown paper and bubble wrap, sent it by boat across the ocean. It feels only right that I hang it in your room—like with this painting, you and Nan are reaching towards one another, touching fingertips. I think if I am to raise you here, we'll need something of my grandmother around.

amethyst (*n. or adj.*) At forty-one weeks, a midwife comes to our house. She asks me to lie on the bed while she sweeps two fingers against my cervix. If all goes well, she says, I can labour in a pool with a view of the hospital's garden. But you do not come that day. Two days later, another midwife tries again. You remain in my body. After a third try, they tell me we will need to induce you to come out. I will need to go to the hospital. They try this twice—and still, you stay inside. The midwives joke that I've made you too comfortable. I have only tried to make you a home.

Two weeks late plus a day—"late" being a relative term, I know—you are pulled from me. Your birth stone was meant to be garnet, but you choose amethyst instead. I should have expected. Your skin is the shade of a purple wine. You have an aching voice, but your eyes are ready for the world. I do not feel ready—for the first minute, I cannot actually believe you are alive at all. But they press your body into my arms and I see that you are breathing. That my blood stains your face and your hair. I know then that you are a wild thing—though you came into this world in a room with no windows, just white walls and fluorescent lights. Outside, I do not know if the grass is bathed in sun or dark. I do not know anything except sensation. They cover your head with a red woollen hat. *Watch over this child*, the colour means.

It is winter, but each day feels long. I am awake through the night while a white moon casts cold light through your window. I want it to be spring, so I can show you the garden. Already there are violet hyacinths pressing themselves from soil.

At every feed, you make a grunting sound, latching hungry to my breast. You do not worry about the room I've chosen, or the plants that are in the garden. I do not tell you that I worry about everything now. That I worry about your breath in the night, about whether I can give you the safety that you need. I worry about making a home here in England—how to teach you love in a country that refuses to acknowledge violence in its past. I do not know how to shake my fear of raising you in a place my father left on purpose. Despite this, I am longing for you to know beauty.

I am worrying too much, so I tell the doctor how worried I am—how my worries feel heavier than a body can hold. He tells me only that I seem to love you, so there is nothing to worry about.

In spring we count the bulbs that have come up around the garden. You and the dog sit together on a playmat while I point to each new thing, giving every plant a name: lavender, rosemary, lilac, heather. Above us the hawthorn leafs out against a pale-blue sky. You watch the play of light and shadow it creates, cooing each time you round your lips and exhale. The world in these moments feels too bright, too tender. Like a bruise.

I cannot know the changes to come.

The solstice passes, and I mark your growth on a chart hung on the wall. I tidy the nursery. The week you push to all fours, a message arrives: we are losing this home.

The rent is rising, and the landlord has lined up newer, richer people to make their lives here. *This is so hard*, they tell us, as though they are the ones losing a home. But there is no negotiation. There is only the number they want, a number we cannot afford. We have eight weeks to go elsewhere.

I do not want to tell you that there are bad people. There will be those who tell you that landlords need to pay their bills, too. But if raising a child is teaching them how to be in this world, then I want to say: *do not be like this*.

Really I am forced to admit how precarious our lives are. We have tried to make you a home, but it is not ours. Shame burns through my body. I don't want to admit that we could be so easily uprooted. I am angry with a system that makes this possible. And angry with myself. I do not expect this anger, or the fear I feel, because it is a stronger feeling than any I've felt before. Stronger even than the worry I've been holding. I now need—more viscerally than I ever needed beauty—to find a home for you.

I cannot tell you where beauty is in a solitary world. The government speaks only of "personal responsibility."

The summer is too hot, and rain never comes. The grass on the common turns straw-bale brown, and dust gathers along the footpath. In July, a heathland burns in the south of England. Grass fires spread across parks in East London. I carry you on my body, hot. I am living with all our worry close to my chest. We have searched for a new home and found nothing. I know we cannot wait much longer.

Each night, you seek my breast in the dark. The rhythm of rooting and latching, rooting and latching is proprioceptive learning. You are making muscle memory, the way I have already learned the light switches in this house, and which floorboards creak too loudly underfoot. I read about separation anxiety and learn that you do not yet know the difference between you and me. Your landscape is my body. The point from which your world extends.

When I am not packing, I take you and the dog on walks along the river and on errands into town. There is so much to organise and so much still unsettled that my stomach feels sick. The doctor tells me that my worry is simply acid, that it can be fixed with tablets. To steady myself, I catalogue every purple thing I find on our walks, making a list in the Notes app of my phone. I say each item aloud to you, though I know you are only just learning to babble sounds. I find a few each day, and with them I see the summer reach its zenith, the heat rising and hardly waning. Lavender, herb Robert, salvia. I outstretch your hand to touch each plant. Along the back lane, thistle is bursting into seed. The yarrow on the common is deepening from cream to mauve. By late August, elderberries are swelling glossy on the branch. Purple hibiscus flowers lean over a brick wall on Clarendon Street, and wisteria is still blooming on the chimney tops of Orchard Street. The wisteria on our front door isn't blooming anymore.

Finding nothing in this town we can afford, that will accept us all, we make the decision to move back to Germany. We are lucky that we can. Your father's work makes this possible. I will have to leave my job, a job I long to keep, but this feels like nothing when placed against the question of home.

In the last days, I take down Nan's painting and wrap it in paper. We pack up the plants in the garden. You crawl from end to end of the house, finding your voice's highest pitch. I pack herbs and tomatoes in containers and salvage what I can of the lavender. We'll take them to Nina in London, to a garden where they can remain. The plants spill over from the boot to the back seat and fill the car with the chlorophyll scent of the life we've uprooted. The heather I do not take with us; it hasn't survived the summer heat.

You cry the entire drive back. I cannot console you, and it doesn't signify anything profound; you just hate the car seat. I watch the sky and tell you what I can see. The sunset glows purple on the motorway ahead. The moon is three-quarters full and is doubled in the passenger side window and the wing mirror. I look to the verge, where rosebay willowherb is growing in full flush. Purple streaked by the speed of our movement.

Malvenfarbe (*n. or adj.*) A week later, we are in the north of Germany, on the northeastern side of Lower Saxony. There is a heathland here. Over a thousand square kilometres in size, it is a little larger than Dartmoor in the south of England. Draw a line between Hamburg and Hannover, and you will find it: Lüneburger Heide.

It is still morning when our train drops us in Schneverdingen, and the light falls from a hard angle in the sky, casting the landscape in pale, bright sun. I am carrying you and a backpack, and a hope that we will find heather.

We are walking into a flat, wide field of sand, with a carpark at one side and an open-pit mine on the other. Beyond the horizon, there is a fur of low trees—pine, birch, and oak—rising from a wave of colour. I cannot describe it with a single word. The entire land here grows thick with heather, and sunlight catches its every tone: russet, pink, purple, white. With the slightest movement, the shade shifts, and I need to look closely again.

We arrived in Germany two days ago, and I have been repeating the words *this is home now*. These are your first days in a new land. I've never been to Lüneburger Heide, though I've always wanted to come. It is famous for its heather. Online there is a dial that shows how fully the heather in the park has saturated, a barometer of its colour and bloom. Between moving vans and registration appointments, we have a free day. So we've come, just to see it. To ask if this place, too, can hold beauty in the way I hope.

It is the largest area of heathland in Central Europe, and Osterheide, where we've come, stretches across the flat western flank of it all. To the east, the landscape is pocketed with hills, but here, flat ground stretches kilometres into the distance.

I do not mistake this place's beauty for neutrality. From the end of the Second World War until the 1990s, it was a military training ground for British and Canadian troops stationed nearby, on land the Nazis took from locals that had, for a time, served also as a postwar refugee camp. In 1959 sections of Lüneburger Heide—"red areas"—were designated for use by my countries' armies. If we do not call this an imperial act, what are we to call it?

In a black-and-white photocopy of a local history book, there are photographs of the land here at the time: pockmarked by the continuous track of tanks, entirely denuded of vegetation. Once the military left, the site's heathland habitat was painstakingly restored.

My feet sink deep into sand when we walk onto it. The path is cut wide for horse-drawn carriages. Some way into the middle of the purple field, the ground compacts and I find a path a little firmer underfoot. Dry summer has left the heather parched and spindly, and though it flames orange and red under the sunlight, everything is clouded by a fine film of sand. This land shows scant evidence of what was here before: the occasional remnant of wood or metal, an information placard, and little else. I cannot entirely picture that it was once filled with tanks. That once, the British military paraded in this region for their queen. Standing in a place rewilded, I know that memory is a slippery thing.

We cut across the heath down a middle path. You are restless after a long journey in the carrier, wriggling and cawing birdlike across an open field. I caw in reply, because I am happy to hear you use your voice. Autumn is breathing into summer, and the sun has begun to beat upon our skin in the cool air. There is almost no shade here—there are pines and larches at the outermost border of the heath, but out in the open space I find only a lanky birch tree to offer shelter. There is a bench nearby, so I settle to breastfeed for a while, listening only to the rhythm of you nursing, the sound of hover flies and bees flitting between the plants. After, I let you free to crawl at my feet, and you plunge your little hands into the margin of the sand.

There is more that grows here than heather, and with you down on ground level I can take some of it in: tansy, with its button-shaped yellow heads, like the buttery centres of daisies. St. John's wort, ragged and dried from a summer in the heat, and very occasionally, the flower from which mauve takes its name: the musk mallow. I count only a few of them, five fine petals in a bell-shaped bloom. Their purple seems more delicate against the surrounding heather, which has grown grey beneath all the colour. Looking out, there isn't just mauve, but a flood of colours, almost pixelated, like the tiny sections of Nan's paint-by-numbers. It never is a single shade.

At the north end of the heath, we follow a path towards a garden. The map tells me it is devoted to heather, to the plant's diversity. There are hundreds of varieties here, all huddled together in tidy, circular beds. You are asleep on my chest, so I can take my time. I walk along the paths, finding my breath, slowing my pace. Each heather plant is labelled with a plastic placard showing its variety. Beneath, each is given a colour, all carefully described to capture the exact quality of that heather's hue.

Until this moment, "Lila" was the only German word I knew for purple. I taught it to you this morning, though you do not yet know words or the beauty they describe. But here I find so many more: "purple red," "violet red," "violet pink," "pink lilac." I shape each shade with my mouth and breathe their names into open air:

Violett
Purpurrot
Hellpurpur
Violettrot
Violettrosa
Lilarosa
Rosalila
Malvenfarbe

—Mauve.

Acknowledgements

MANY OF THE ESSAYS IN THIS BOOK BEGAN LIFE in a *Catapult* magazine column called "Non-Native Species." Allisen Lichtenstein, my editor on the column, shaped my thinking and writing enormously—I am beyond grateful. This book would not exist without her.

Enormous thanks to my editors Nicole Winstanley, Simon Prosser, Summer Farah, and Tajja Isen. And to David Godwin and the team at DGA. Your belief in this collection has been invaluable.

Thanks to Helen Anne Curry, Ryan Nehring, Tad Brown, Daniela Sclavo, João Joaquim, Hitesh Pant, Erinn Campbell, Leo Chu, Zsuzsanna Ihar, Emiliano Cabrera Rocha, Theo Di Castri, Xan Chacko, Katie Dow, and all who implicitly and explicitly shaped my thinking and writing while at Cambridge HPS. To my colleagues and students at Cambridge ICE for encouragement and inspiration.

Thanks to Rachel Hopwood, Alyssa Mackenzie, Jennifer Neal, and Dasom Yang for unconditional cheerleading. To Becky Allen for time on the allotment. To Zaffar Kunial for that day in Haworth. To Rowan Hisayo Buchanan and Nina Mingya Powles: thank you for walks, plants, talks, food, and friendship.

This book was completed in the late months of pregnancy and the first year of my daughter's life. I could not have finished it without the support of my husband, Ricardo, who gave me time, freedom, and unfathomable belief when I needed it most. Thank you.

Notes

A Note to the Reader

"'Metaphors are always a double bind.'": Andreas Hejnol, "Ladders, Trees, Complexity, and Other Metaphors in Evolutionary Thinking," in *Arts of Living on a Damaged Planet: Ghosts*, eds. Anna Tsing, Heather Swanson, Elaine Gan, and Nils Bubandt (Minneapolis: University of Minnesota Press, 2017), G87–G102.

1. Margin

"Early studies suggest": Michael L. Moody, Nayell Palomino, Philip S. R. Weyl, Julie A. Coetzee, Raymond M. Newman, Nathan E. Harms, Xing Liu, and Ryan A. Thum, "Unraveling the Biogeographic Origins of the Eurasian Watermilfoil (*Myriophyllum spicatum*) Invasion in North America," *American Journal of Botany* 103, no. 4 (2016): 709–18.

"one of the first species to slowly recolonise the lake": Sabine Hilt, Jan Köhler, Rita Adrian, Michael T. Monaghan, and Carl D. Sayer, "Clear, Crashing, Turbid and Back—Long-Term Changes in Macrophyte Assemblages in a Shallow Lake," *Freshwater Biology* 58, no. 10 (2013): 2027–36.

"the list of countries it calls home": POWO, "Stuckenia pectinata (L.) Börner," in *Plants of the World Online*, facilitated by the

Royal Botanic Gardens at Kew, retrieved November 21, 2022. powo.science.kew.org/taxon/urn:lsid:ipni.org:names:77099639-1.

"Measures to control the movement of plants across borders": Christina Devorshak, *Plant Pest Risk Analysis: Concepts and Applications* (Wallingford: CABI, 2022), 22.

"In a 2018 study": Céline Albert, Gloria M. Luque, Franck Courchamp, "The Twenty Most Charismatic Species," *PLoS ONE* 13, no. 7 (2018): e0199149.

"the city proposes to transform a freshwater ditch": "Jesus Ditch Biodiversity Enhancements Consultation," Cambridge City Council, September 7, 2021. www.cambridge .gov.uk/consultations/jesus-ditch-biodiversity-enhancements -consultation.

"the species of the riparian zone": C. D. Preston, "The Aquatic Plants of the River Cam and Its Riparian Commons, Cambridge, 1660–1999," *Nature in Cambridgeshire* 50 (2008): 18–37.

2. Border Trees

"ten thousand cherry trees in total were gifted": "Kirschbluten in Berlin," Berlin.de, updated April 19, 2022. www.berlin.de /tourismus/insidertipps/5263242-2339440-kirschblueten-in -berlin.html.

"fruiting European cultivars" and "hardy North American timber cherries": Gayle Brandow Samuels, *Enduring Roots: Encounters with Trees, History, and the American Landscape* (New Brunswick, NJ: 2005), 69–70.

"Sato-zakura, 'village cherries'": Roland M. Jefferson and Kay Kazue Wain, "The Nomenclature of Cultivated Japanese Flowering Cherries (Prunus): The Sato-zakura Group," *National Arboretum Contribution* 5 (1984), 3.

"'one of the most ornamental hardy plants with which I am acquainted'": John Lindley, "Report Upon New or Rare Plants, etc.," *Transactions of the Horticultural Society of London* (1830): 239.

"'like thin flakes of snow'": Robert Fortune, *Yedo and Peking: A Narrative of a Journey to the Capitals of Japan and China* (London: John Murray, 1863), 83–84.

"Recounting a visit to Japan in 1907": Marie C. Stopes, *A Journal from Japan: A Daily Record of Life as Seen by a Scientist* (London: Blackie and Son, 1910), 131, 134.

"described the trees as 'superlatively lovely'": Collingwood Ingram, *Ornamental Cherries* (London: Country Life Limited, 1948), 13, 21; Naoko Abe, *Cherry Ingram: The Englishman Who Saved Japan's Blossoms* (London: Vintage, 2019).

"an 1893 handbook for young Japanese botanists": Kōtarō Saida and Akiomi Tokahashi, *An Elementary Text-book of Botany, for the Use of Japanese Students* (Tokyo: 1893), 2.

"'the queen/king of flowers in Japanese'": Emiko Ohnuki-Tierney, *Kamikaze, Cherry Blossoms, and Nationalisms: The Militarization of Aesthetics in Japanese History* (Chicago: University of Chicago Press, 2002), 10.

"'The master trope of Japan's imperial nationalism'": Ohnuki-Tierney, 3.

"Nishi Amane explicitly positioned the cherry blossom in opposition to the peony and rose": Ohnuki-Tierney, 107.

"The environmental historian Alfred Crosby famously argued": Alfred W. Crosby, *Ecological Imperialism: The Biological Expansion of Europe, 900–1900* (Cambridge: Cambridge University Press, 2004 [1986]).

"the British East India Company's botanical gardens": Ramesh Kannan, Charlie M. Shackleton, and R. Uma Shaanker,

"Reconstructing the History of Introduction and Spread of the Invasive Species, *Lantana*, at Three Spatial Scales in India," *Biological Invasions* 15, no. 3 (2013): 1287–1302.

"**Lauret Savoy writes in her exquisite memoir**": Lauret Savoy, *Trace: Memory, History, Race, and the American Landscape* (Berkeley: Counterpoint Press, 2015), 86.

"**Japanese scientists have been collating data**": Richard Primack and Hiroyoshi Higuchi, "Climate Change and Cherry Tree Blossom Festivals in Japan," *Arnoldia* 65, no. 1 (2007): 14–22.

"**Japanese cherry blossom festivals go back much further than usual datasets**": Richard Primack, Hiroyoshi Higuchi, and Abraham J. Miller-Rushing, "The Impact of Climate Change on Cherry Trees and Other Species in Japan," *Biological Conservation* 142, no. 9 (2009): 1943–49.

"**the cherries began consistently flowering earlier**": Brittany Patterson, "Cherry Blossoms May Bloom Earlier Than Ever This Year," *Scientific American*, March 2, 2017. www.scientificamerican.com/article/cherry-blossoms-may-bloom-earlier-than-ever-this-year/.

3. Frontier

"**the basement of the home as a space of irrational dreaming**": Gaston Bachelard, *The Poetics of Space*, trans. Maria Jolas (Boston: Beacon Press, 1994), 18.

"**to visit Java, to understand plants and their pathologies in place**": Daniel Stone, *The Food Explorer: The True Adventures of the Globe-Trotting Botanist Who Transformed What America Eats* (New York: Dutton, 2018), 20.

"**'But there I was, with an adventure on my hands'**": David Fairchild, *The World Was My Garden* (New York: Charles Scribner's Sons, 1938), 47.

"He asks permission instead to become a 'special agent'": Fairchild, 117.

"a well-lighted laboratory for microscopical work": David Fairchild, "Two Expeditions after Living Plants," *The Scientific Monthly* 26, no. 2 (1928): 98–99.

"Frederick Wilson Popenoe": Allan Stoner, "19th and 20th Century Plant Hunters," *Horticultural Science* 42, no. 2 (2007): 197–99.

"One of the founding missions of the USDA": The Organic Act of 1862, Ch. 72, § 1, 12 Stat. 387 (May 15, 1862).

"essential for cultivation and settlement": Tiago Saraiva, "Cloning as Orientalism: Reproducing Citrus in Mandatory Palestine," in *Nature Remade: Engineering Life, Envisioning Worlds*, ed. Luis A. Campos, Michael R. Dietrich, Tiago Saraiva, and Christian C. Young (Chicago: University of Chicago Press, 2021), 45.

"'plant immigrants'": USDA Foreign Seed and Plant Introduction, "Plant Immigrants," no. 153 (January 1919), National Agricultural Library Digital Collections.

"The captions are written by Fairchild himself": USDA Bureau of Plant Industry, "Agricultural Explorations in Ceylon, Sumatra and Java," 1925–26, Special Collections of the USDA National Agricultural Library, film: captions from 00:24 and 12:55.

"the captions speak of wayfaring, enterprising voyagers": USDA Bureau of Plant Industry, "Naturalized Plant Immigrants," 1929, Special Collections of the USDA National Agricultural Library, film: caption from 00:30.

"In one scene he is asking to be ordained as a monk": Fairchild, *The World Was My Garden*, 40.

"an obituary of Yamei Kin": Mike Ives, "Overlooked No More: Yamei Kin, the Chinese Doctor Who Introduced Tofu to the West," *The New York Times*, October 17, 2018.

"A full-page spread in *The New York Times Magazine*": "Woman Off to China as Government Agent to Study Soy Bean; Dr. Kin Will Make Report for United States on the Most Useful Food of Her Native Land," *The New York Times Magazine*, June 10, 1917, Section T, 65.

"A woman who was celebrated for her expertise": William Shurtleff and Akiko Aoyagi, "Biography of Yamei Kin M.D. (1864–1934), (Also known as Jin Yunmei), the First Chinese Woman to Take a Medical Degree in the United States (1864-2016): Extensively Annotated Bio-Bibliography, 2nd ed. with McCartee Family Genealogy and Knight Family Genealogy" (Lafayette, CA: Soyinfo Center, 2016).

"the Orient": Edward W. Said, *Orientalism* (London: Routledge, 1980 [1978]).

"the plants for whose introduction he can be credited": Karen Williams and Gayle M. Volk, "The USDA Plant Introduction Program," in *Crop Wild Relatives in Genebanks*, eds. Gayle M. Volk and Patrick F. Byrne (Fort Collins, Colorado: Colorado State University, 2020). colostate.pressbooks.pub/cropwild relatives/chapter/usda-plant-introduction-program/.

"Kew researchers train those on the ground": Xan Sarah Chacko, "Creative Practices of Care: The Subjectivity, Agency, and Affective Labor of Preparing Seeds for Long-term Banking," *Culture, Agriculture, Food, and Environment* 41, no. 2 (2019): 100.

"began to repatriate plant specimen data": The National Commission for the Knowledge and Use of Biodiversity, "Repatriation of Plant Specimens Data from the Botanical Garden of New York Herbarium." www.conabio.gob.mx/remib_ingles /doctos/jbny.html.

"digital records of plants have been repatriated to a Brazilian archive": Reflora, "Virtual Herbarium." reflora.jbrj.gov.br /reflora/herbarioVirtual/.

"restoring species to the Indigenous communities": Native Seeds/SEARCH. www.nativeseeds.org.

4. Sweetness

"may never have actually seen a mango tree for himself": André Joseph Guillaume Henri Kostermans, Jean-Marie Bompard, International Board for Plant Genetic Resources, and Linnean Society of London, *The Mangoes: Their Botany, Nomenclature, Horticulture and Utilization* (London: Academic, 1993), 21.

"more recent genetic analysis": Emily J. Warschefsky and Eric J. B. von Wettberg, "Population Genomic Analysis of Mango (*Mangifera indica*) Suggests a Complex History of Domestication," *New Phytologist* 222, no. 4 (2019): 2023–37.

"the story of the fruit": S. K. Mukherjee, "Origin of Mango (*Mangifera indica*)," *Economic Botany* 26, no. 3 (1972): 260–64.

"these Floridian mangoes dominate": CBI, "The European Market Potential for Mangoes," updated December 21, 2021. www.cbi.eu/market-information/fresh-fruit-vegetables/mangoes /market-potential.

"In E. M. Forster's 1924 novel": E. M. Forster, *A Passage to India* (London: Penguin, 1952 [1924]), 72, 117.

"In a 1964 essay": V. S. Naipaul, "Jasmine: Words to Play With," *Times Literary Supplement*, June 4, 1964. www.the-tls.co.uk /articles/words-to-play-with/.

"the opening lines of Arundhati Roy's 1997 novel": Arundhati Roy, *The God of Small Things* (London: 4th Estate, 2017 [1997]) 1; Rana Dasgupta, "A New Bend in the River," *The National*,

February 25, 2010. www.thenationalnews.com/arts-culture/a -new-bend-in-the-river-1.541963.

"the writer Jeet Thayil proclaimed": Jeet Thayil, "'Narcopolis': Inside India's Dark Underbelly," NPR, April 8, 2012. www.npr .org/2012/04/08/150003126/wesun-narcopolis-shell.

"the Swedish American daughter of a California rancher": Saskia Vogel, "The Mango King," *Catapult*, November 18, 2015. catapult.co/stories/the-mango-king.

"The ban decimated sales of Alphonsos that year": BBC, "UK 'Working to End' Ban on Indian Mango Imports," *BBC News*, April 28, 2014. www.bbc.co.uk/news/uk-politics-27185683.

"Dianne Jacob, in her 2016 essay": Dianne Jacob, "The Meaning of Mangoes," *Lucky Peach*, 2016. web.archive.org/web/20170702 004942/http://luckypeach.com/the-meaning-of-mangoes/.

"The Japanese American cartoonist Sam Nakahira writes": Sam Nakahira, "My Grandparent's Hawaiian Mangoes," *Asian American Writers Workshop: The Margins*, December 6, 2019. aaww.org/hawaiian-mangoes-sam-nakahira/.

"in an essay called 'Consequences of Water'": K-Ming Chang, "Consequences of Water," *Asian American Writers Workshop: The Margins*, December 9, 2019. aaww.org/consequences-of-water/.

5. Tidal

"women who spent their days cataloguing algae": Anne B. Shteir, *Cultivating Women, Cultivating Science: Flora's Daughters and Botany in England, 1760–1860* (Baltimore: Johns Hopkins University Press, 1996).

"Anna Atkins was raised amidst the scientific milieu": Shteir, 177.

"her writings as a result centre seaweeds": Isabella Gifford, *The Marine Botanist: An Introduction to the Study of Algology* (London: Darton and Co., 1848).

"she was herself described by the *Journal of Botany* as part of an essential circle": "Isabella Gifford," *Journal of Botany* 30 (1892), 81.

"Sticks, she wrote, were ideal appendages": Margaret Scott Gatty, *British Sea-Weeds*, Volume I (London: Bell and Daldy, 1872), ix.

"Drew-Baker's research": Kathleen M. Drew, "Conchocelis-Phase in the Life-History of Porphyra umbilicalis (L.) Kütz," *Nature* 164 (1949): 748–49.

"scientists turn to remote sensing": Juliet Brodie, Lauren V. Ash, Ian Tittley, and Chris Yesson, "A Comparison of Multispectral Aerial and Satellite Imagery for Mapping Intertidal Seaweed Communities," *Aquatic Conservation: Marine and Freshwater Ecosystems* 28, no. 4 (2018): 872–81.

"according to the EPA's blog": EPA, "Japanese Tsunami Debris and Potential Invasions in Western North America," *Perspectives*, June 29, 2012.

"The dock had been 'cut loose'": Richard Read, "Huge Dock Washed Ashore on Oregon Coast is Debris from Japan's Tsunami," *Oregon Live*, June 6, 2012. www.oregonlive.com/pacific-north west-news/2012/06/huge_dock_washed_ashore_on_ore.html.

"lists of the species recorded as having made the five-thousand-mile journey": Gayle I. Hansen, Takeaki Hanyuda, and Hiroshi Kawai, "Invasion Threat of Benthic Marine Algae Arriving on Japanese Tsunami Marine Debris in Oregon and Washington, USA," *Phycologia* 57, no. 6 (2018), 641–58.

"a collaged image of the species": "Marine Organisms Found on Agate Beach, OR Floating Dock," *Biota on Japanese Tsunami Marine Debris*, Oregon State University Blogs, July 30, 2012. blogs.oregonstate.edu/floatingdock/2012/07/30 /marine-organisms-found-on-floating-dock/.

"I read about the Japanese shore crab": Bob Ward, "Oregon Authorities to Demolish Japanese Tsunami Dock," *The Guardian*, July 30, 2012. www.theguardian.com/environment/2012/jul/30/japan-tsunami-dock-wildlife.

"the species is classed as being amongst the world's worst invasive species": Hansen, Hanyuda, and Kawai, "Invasion Threat of Benthic Marine Algae," 641.

"wakame is now a species with a 'global nonnative range'": Graham Epstein and Dan A. Smale, *"Undaria pinnatifida*: A Case Study to Highlight Challenges in Marine Invasion Ecology and Management," *Ecology and Evolution* 7, no. 20 (2017): 8624.

"kelp forests are disappearing": Alastair Bland, "As Oceans Warm, the World's Kelp Forests Begin to Disappear," *Yale Environment 360*, November 20, 2017. e360.yale.edu/features/as-oceans-warm-the-worlds-giant-kelp-forests-begin-to-disappear.

"century-old seaweed samples have been used to extract data": Laura Trethewey, "What Victorian-Era Seaweed Pressings Reveal About Our Changing Seas," *The Guardian*, October 27, 2020. www.theguardian.com/environment/2020/oct/27/what-victorian-era-seaweed-pressings-reveal-about-our-changing-seas.

"several species of seaweed made their way into the hearths of humans": Tom D. Dillehay, C. Ramírez M. Pino, M. B. Collins, J. Rossen, and J. D. Pino-Navarro, "Monte Verde: Seaweed, Food, Medicine, and the Peopling of South America," *Science* 320, no. 5877 (2008): 784–86.

"Zuo Si wrote of tsu-tsai": Li-En Yang, Qin-Qin Lu, and Juliet Brodie, "A Review of the Bladed Bangiales (Rhodophyta) in China: History, Culture and Taxonomy," *European Journal of Phycology* 52, no. 3 (2017): 251–63.

"seaweeds described by journalists": Adrienne Murray, "Seaweed: The Food and Fuel of the Future?," *BBC News*, August 27, 2020. www.bbc.co.uk/news/business-53610683.

"They serve as fodder for potential biofuels": Maya Glicksman and Olivia Hemond, "Taking Carbon Farming Out to Sea," *Carbon180*, August 10, 2020. carbon180.medium.com /taking-carbon-farming-out-to-sea-60a7f7626fa5.

"proteins from algae have been genetically manipulated": Fiona Harvey, "Gene Manipulation Using Algae Could Grow More Crops with Less Water," *The Guardian*, August 10, 2020. www .theguardian.com/environment/2020/aug/10/gene-manipulation -using-algae-could-grow-more-crops-with-less-water.

"In Singapore, an entrepreneur builds a vertical algae farm": Rob Fletcher, "High-Five: Developing 'the World's First Vertical Aquaculture Farm,'" *The Fish Site*, November 24, 2020. thefishsite.com/articles/high-five-developing-the-worlds-first -vertical-aquaculture-farm.

"a 'scalable climate change' solution": United Nations Environment Programme, *Seaweed Farming: Assessment on the Potential of Sustainable Upscaling for Climate, Communities and the Planet* (Nairobi: UNEP, 2023).

"The language around seaweed farming": Maggie Rulli, "How an Underwater Solution in the Faroe Islands Could Combat Climate Change," ABC News, November 4, 2021. youtu.be /Zo2rQiV3PFk.

"enterprising fishermen seeking livelihoods beyond fish": Bren Smith, "The Seas Will Save Us: How an Army of Ocean Farmers are Starting an Economic Revolution," *Medium*, March 25, 2016. medium.com/invironment/an-army-of-ocean-farmers-on-the -frontlines-of-the-blue-green-economic-revolution-d5ae171285a3.

"It has been described as perhaps the most successful invasive": John J. Milledge, Birthe V. Nielsen, and David Bailey, "High-Value Products from Macroalgae: The Potential Uses of the Invasive Brown Seaweed, *Sargassum muticum*," *Reviews in Environmental Science and Bio/technology* 15 (2016): 67–88.

6. Words for Tea

"The tree is thought to have originated": George L. van Driem, *The Tale of Tea: A Comprehensive History of Tea from Prehistoric Times to the Present Day* (Leiden: Brill, 2019), 1, 7.

"ornamental camellias share a long history of confusion with the tea plant": Nicholas K. Menzies, "Representations of the Camellia in China and During Its Early Career in the West," *Curtis's Botanical Magazine* 34, no. 4 (2017): 458. www.jstor.org/stable/48505843.

"demand for opium traded by the British East India Company facilitated British access": van Driem, *The Tale of Tea*, 603.

"Britain was reliant upon this trade": Lucile Brockway, *Science and Colonial Expansion: The Role of the British Royal Botanic Gardens* (New Haven: Yale UP, 2002 [1979]).

"By 1839 . . . Britain was embroiled in the first Opium War": G. G. Sigmond, *Tea: Its Effects, Medicinal and Moral* (London: Longman, Orme, Brown, Green, & Longmans, 1839), 2.

"largely through indentured labour": Justin Rowlatt, "The Dark History Behind India and the UK's Favourite Drink," *BBC News*, July 15, 2016. www.bbc.co.uk/news/world-asia-india-36781368.

"Fortune donned a disguise": Robert Fortune, *A Journey to the Tea Countries of China* (Cambridge: Cambridge University Press, 2012 [1852]), 22–25.

"'No dependence can be placed upon the veracity of the Chinese'": Fortune, 21.

"in one popular history by Sarah Rose": Sarah Rose, *For All the Tea in China: How England Stole the World's Favourite Drink and Changed History* (New York: Penguin, 2011).

"in a biography of Fortune": Alistair Watt and D. J. Mabberley, *Robert Fortune: A Plant Hunter in the Orient* (Richmond: Kew, 2017), xix.

"the words of historian Lucile Brockway": Brockway, *Science and Colonial Expansion*, 28; Francesca Bray, Barbara Hahn, John Bosco Lourdusamy, and Tiago Saraiva, "Cropscapes and History: Reflections on Rootedness and Mobility," *Transfers: Interdisciplinary Journal of Mobility Studies* 9, no. 1 (2019): 22.

"thinking of U.S. history, tea has signified rebellion": Erling Hoh and Victor H. Mair, *The True History of Tea* (New York: Thames and Hudson, 2009).

"In sixteenth-century Japan": Cathy Kaufmann, "A Simple Bowl of Tea: Power Politics and Aesthetics in Hideyoshi's Japan, 1582–1591," *Dublin Gastronomy Symposium* (2018).

"in 1920s Iran": Helen Saberi, *Tea: A Global History* (London: Reaktion, 2010), 72.

"at odds with sustaining local ecologies": Annesha Chowdhury, Abhishek Samrat, M. Soubadra Devy, "Can Tea Support Biodiversity with a Few 'Nudges' in Management: Evidence from Tea Growing Landscapes Around the World," *Global Ecology and Conservation* 31 (2021). doi.org/10.1016/j.gecco.2021.e01801.

"other species of the *Camellia* genus face habitat loss": van Driem, *The Tale of Tea*, 18.

"precarious labour practices on tea plantations": William McLennan, "Environmental Damage and Human Rights Abuses Blight Global Tea Sector," *The Ecologist*, April 13, 2011; Jill Didur, "Reimagining the Plantation (ocene): Mulk Raj Anand's *Two Leaves and a Bud*," *Postcolonial Studies* 25, no. 3 (2021): 340–60.

"There's a famous saying": Nikhil Sonnad, "Tea If By Sea, Cha If By Land: Why the World Only Has Two Words for Tea," *Quartz*, January 11, 2018. qz.com/1176962/map-how-the-word -tea-spread-over-land-and-sea-to-conquer-the-world/.

"one of the most comprehensive recent histories of tea": van Driem, *The Tale of Tea*.

7. Dispersals

"'the most dangerous plant in Britain'": Charlie Duffield and Lowenna Waters, "What Is Giant Hogweed? How to Identify and Get Rid of Britain's 'Most Dangerous Plant,'" *Evening Standard*, August 12, 2022.

"brought to Western Europe as an ornamental": *"Heracleum mantegazzianum* (Giant Hogweed)," *Invasive Species Compendium*, CABI, September 30, 2007 [updated April 30, 2014]. www.cabi.org/isc/datasheet/26911.

"one of my favourite books about plants": Richard Mabey, *Weeds* (London: Profile Books, 2010), 1.

"'the sun never sets on the empire of the dandelion'": Alfred Crosby, *Ecological Imperialism* (Cambridge: Cambridge University Press, 1986), 7.

"'a plant in the wrong place'": Mabey, *Weeds*, 5.

"tidy definition of 'dirt'": Mary Douglas, *Purity and Danger* (London: Routledge, 2001 [1966]), 36.

"'It is the existence of some system of classification...'": Harriet Ritvo, "At the Edge of the Garden: Nature and Domestication in Eighteenth- and Nineteenth-Century Britain," *Huntington Library Quarterly* 55, no. 3 (1992): 363.

"the hogweed will move northward": Quadri A. Anibaba, Marcin K. Dyderski, and Andrzej M. Jagodziński, "Predicted

Range Shifts of Invasive Giant Hogweed (*Heracleum mantegazzianum*) in Europe," *Science of the Total Environment* 825 (2022), 154053.

"Watson described plants in Britain as *native, denizen, colonist, alien,* or *incognita*": He also included a label for Irish and Channel Islands plants, which he excluded from the volume. Hewett Cottrell Watson, *Cybele Britannica: or British Plants and their geographical relations* (London: Longman and Co., 1847), 63–64.

"'Arrangement is the first effort of science'": Watson, 20.

"categories of *cultivated, adventitious, recently naturalised, formerly naturalised,* and *primitive* or *aboriginal*": Alphonse de Candolle, *Géographie botanique raisonnée; ou, Exposition des faits principaux et des lois concernant la distribution géographique des plantes de l'époque actuelle* (Paris: V Masson, 1855), 611.

"unavoidably' be classed as native": Matthew K. Chew and Andrew L. Hamilton, "The Rise and Fall of Biotic Nativeness: A Historical Perspective," in *Fifty Years of Invasion Ecology: The Legacy of Charles Elton*, ed. David M. Richardson (Oxford: Blackwell, 2011), 39–40.

"what he termed a 'breakdown' of Wallace's realms": Charles Elton, *The Ecology of Invasions by Animals and Plants*, 2nd Edition (Oxford: Springer, 2020), 38.

"'setting up terrific dislocations in nature'": Elton, 10.

"too reminiscent of war": Elton, x.

"of the 1992 Convention on Biological Diversity": The Convention on Biological Diversity of June 5, 1992 (1760 U.N.T.S. 69), Article 8(h); Benji Jones, "Why the US Won't Join the Single Most Important Treaty to Protect Nature," *Vox*, May 20, 2021. www.vox.com/22434172/us-cbd-treaty -biological-diversity-nature-conservation.

"noting the ways the plants themselves are obfuscated": Banu Subramaniam, "The Aliens Have Landed! Reflections on the Rhetoric of Biological Invasions," *Meridians* 2, no. 1 (2001): 28; Banu Subramaniam, "Spectacles of Belonging: (Un)documenting Citizenship in a Multispecies World," in *The Ethics and Rhetoric of Invasion Ecology*, eds. James Stanescu and Kevin Cummings (Lanham: Lexington Books, 2016), 87–102.

"the legacy of a Nazi obsession": Eric Katz, "The Nazi Comparison in the Debate over Restoration: Nativism and Domination," *Environmental Values* 23, no. 4 (2014): 377–98.

"this debate": David Simberloff, "Confronting Introduced Species: A Form of Xenophobia?," *Biological Invasions* 5 (2003): 179–92; James C. Russell and Tim M. Blackburn, "The Rise of Invasive Species Denialism," *Trends in Ecology and Evolution* 32, no. 1 (2017): 1–3; Mark A. Davis and Matthew K. Chew, "'The Denialists Are Coming!' Well, Not Exactly: A Response to Russell and Blackburn," *Trends in Ecology and Evolution* 32, no. 4 (2017): 229–30.

"survey of plants": Kevin Walker, Peter Stroh, Tom Humphrey, David Roy, Richard Burkmar, and Oliver Pescott, *Britain's Changing Flora: A Summary of the Results of* Plant Atlas 2020, (Durham: Botanical Society of Britain and Ireland, 2023), 2.

"'Introduced species' and categories": Robert I. Colautti and Hugh J. MacIsaac, "A Neutral Terminology to Define 'Invasive' Species," *Diversity and Distribution* 10, no. 2 (2004): 135–41.

"propose to do away with the 'immigrant' status": Charles R. Warren, "Perspectives on the 'Alien' Versus 'Native' Species Debate: A Critique of Concepts, Language and Practice," *Progress in Human Geography* 31, no. 4 (2007): 436–37.

8. Bitter Greens

"**brassicas provide a greater diversity**": Geoffrey R. Dixon, *Vegetable Brassicas and Related Crucifers* (Wallingford: CABI, 2007), 2.

"**Its value has crossed cultures and continents**": Lorenzo Maggioni, Roland von Bothmer, Gert Poulsen, and Ferdinando Branca, "Origin and Domestication of Cole Crops (*Brassica oleracea L.*): Linguistic and Literary Considerations," *Economic Botany* 64, no. 2 (2010): 118; NordGen, "Brassica rapa," Plant Portraits, 2020. www.nordgen.org/en/plant-portraits/brassica-rapa/.

"**Chinese records**": Chia Wen Li, "The Origin, Evolution, Taxonomy and Hybridization of Chinese Cabbage," in *Chinese Cabbage: Proceedings of the First International Symposium*, eds. N. S. Talekar and T. D. Griggs (Shanhua, Taiwan: Asian Vegetable Research and Development Center, 1981), 3–10.

"**Searches through the genome**": Xinshuai Qi, Hong An, Aaron P. Ragsdale, Tara E. Hall, Ryan N. Gutenkunst, J. Chris Pires, and Michael S. Barker, "Genomic Inferences of Domestication Events are Corroborated by Written Records in *Brassica rapa*," *Molecular Ecology* 26 (2017): 3383.

"**a relatively shorter history**": Lorenzo Maggioni, Roland von Bothmer, Gert Poulsen, and Elinor Lipman. "Domestication, Diversity and Use of Brassica oleracea L., Based on Ancient Greek and Latin Texts," *Genetic Resources and Crop Evolution* 65 (2018): 137–59.

"**researchers remain uncertain**": Alex C. McAlvay, Aaron P. Ragsdale, Makenzie E. Mabry, Xinshuai Qi, Kevin A. Bird, Pablo Velasco, Hong An, J. Chris Pires, and Eve Emshwiller, "*Brassica rapa* Domestication: Untangling Wild and Feral Forms and Convergence of Crop Morphotypes," *Molecular Biology and Evolution* 38, no. 8 (2021): 3359.

"plants are 'willing partners'": Michael Pollan, *The Botany of Desire* (New York: Random House, 2002), xxv.

"a variety of stem broccoli was developed": Russ Parsons, "Aspiration: Asparation," *Los Angeles Times*, March 18, 1998. www .latimes.com/archives/la-xpm-1998-mar-18-fo-29958-story.html.

9. Bean

"the bean is the subject of verse": "Cai Shu" in *The Chinese Classics (Shī jīng - The Book of Odes)*, Volume 4, trans. James Legge (Taipei: SMC, 2000). Online version of the text available via the University of Virginia Chinese Text Initiative: cti.lib.virginia .edu/shijing/AnoShih.html.

"blocks of tofu are likened to white jade": 苏轼 (Su Shi), 東坡樂府 (Dongpo Yuefu). Produced by Geast Huang, Project Gutenberg EBook (2007). www.gutenberg.org/cache/epub/24028 /pg24028.html.

"pools of soy pulp become snow": 孫作 (Sun Zuo), "菽乳" ("Shu Ru"), 中華古詩文古書籍網. Chinese Ancient Poetry and Classical Books Network. www.arteducation.com.tw/shiwenv _cdb36769152b.html.

"a handful of odes to tofu": William Shurtleff and Akiko Aoyagi, *History of Tofu and Tofu Products (965 CE to 2013): Extensively Annotated Bibliography and Sourcebook* (Lafayette, CA: Soy Info Center, 2013).

"Oil crops were used in the manufacture": Ines Prodöhl, "Versatile and Cheap: A Global History of Soy in the First Half of the Twentieth Century," *Journal of Global History* 8, no. 3 (2013): 461–82.

"transactions mostly facilitated by Japanese agents": Prodöhl, "Versatile and Cheap"; David Wolff, "Bean There: A Soy-Based

History of Northeast Asia," *The South Atlantic Quarterly* 99, no. 1 (2000): 241–52.

"the USDA had grown and experimented": USDA, *Soy Bean* (Washington, D.C.: Government Printing Office, 1920), 3.

"Ford opened a soybean research laboratory": Jim McCabe, "Soybeans: Henry Ford's Miracle Crop," *The Henry Ford*, November 17, 2014. www.thehenryford.org/explore/blog/soybeans; Soybean Lab Agricultural Gallery, The Collections of the Henry Ford, Object 29.3051.1. www.thehenryford.org/collections-and -research/digital-collections/artifact/83790#slide=gs-218675.

"soy oil stepped in to fill the gap": Prodöhl, "Versatile and Cheap," 478; Ines Prodöhl, "From Dinner to Dynamite: Fats and Oils in Wartime America," *Global Food History* 2, no. 1 (2016): 31–50.

"more soy was grown on home soil": Prodöhl, "Versatile and Cheap," 463.

"soybeans were genetically modified": FDA, "GMO Crops, Animal Food, and Beyond," U.S. Food and Drug Administration, February 17, 2022. www.fda.gov/food/agricultural-biotechnology /gmo-crops-animal-food-and-beyond.

"'I feel sad for the person who wrote this'": Nina Mingya Powles, "Tofu Heart," in *Small Bodies of Water* (Edinburgh: Canongate, 2021), 180. First published in *Vittles* 2.8, April 29, 2020. vittles .substack.com/p/vittles-28-making-doufu-hua?s=r.

"exploration of the virtues of soybeans as livestock feed": Walter Fitch Ingalls, *Soy Beans* (Cooperstown, NY: The Arthur H. Crist Co., 1912), 8.

"'consuming soybeans in an Asian manner'": Prodöhl, "Versatile and Cheap," 474.

"campaigners against it framed it as a dangerous 'propaganda food'": Julia McKinnell, "Will Soy Make My Son Gay?," *Maclean's*, December 4, 2008. www.macleans.ca/society

/health/will-soy-make-my-son-gay/; Faye Flam, "Oh, Boy! Do Guys Need to Worry About Soy?," *The Seattle Times*, January 14, 2007. www.seattletimes.com/seattle-news/health/oh-boy-do-guys-need-to-worry-about-soy/.

"the bean was cast as a source of all manner of ailments": "Straight Talk About Soy," *The Nutrition Source - Harvard T. Chan School of Public Health*, accessed May 5, 2020. www.hsph.harvard.edu/nutritionsource/soy/.

"stereotypes and patriarchal fears": James Hamblin, "Why Men Think Plant-Based Meat Will Turn Them Into Women," *The Atlantic*, February 3, 2020. www.theatlantic.com/health/archive/2020/02/why-men-are-afraid-soy-will-turn-them-women/605968/.

"In alt-right parlance": Iselin Gambert and Tobias Linné, "From Rice Eaters to Soy Boys: Race, Gender, and Tropes of 'Plant Food Masculinity,'" *Animal Studies Journal* 7, no. 2 (2018): 129–79.

"Why Silk wasn't at all what I knew soy milk to be": Clarissa Wei, "How America Killed Soy Milk," *Eater*, February 15, 2016. www.eater.com/2016/2/15/10995808/america-soymilk-fresh.

10. Sour Fruit

"citrus groves covered nearly a million acres of Florida": Christian Warren, "'Nature's Navels': An Overview of the Many Environmental Histories of Florida Citrus," in *Paradise Lost?: The Environmental History of Florida*, eds. Raymond Arsenault and Jack E. Davis (Gainesville: University Press of Florida, 2005), 179.

"Their origin point is a red star": Guohong Albert Wu, Javier Terol, Victoria Ibanez, et al., "Genomics of the Origin and Evolution of Citrus," *Nature* 554 (2018): 311–16. doi.org/10.1038/nature25447.

"The names we use contain a trace of this past": Dorian Q. Fuller, et al., "Charred Pummelo Peel, Historical Linguistics and Other Tree Crops: Approaches to Framing the Historical Context of Early Citrus Cultivation in East, South and Southeast Asia," in *Agrumed: Archaeology and History of Citrus Fruit in the Mediterranean: Acclimatization, Diversifications, Uses*, eds. Véronique Zech-Matterne and Girolamo Fiorentino (Naples: Publications du Centre Jean Bérard, 2017). books.openedition.org/pcjb/2173.

"a word I've borrowed": Wu, Terol, Ibanez, et al., "Genomics of the Origin and Evolution of Citrus."

"akin to blending primary colours": Dan Nosowitz, "Grapefruit Is One of the Weirdest Fruits on the Planet," *Gastro Obscura*, October 6, 2020. www.atlasobscura.com/articles /grapefruit-history-and-drug-interactions.

"by way of trade over land through present-day Iran and Iraq": L. Ramón-Laca, "The Introduction of Cultivated Citrus to Europe via Northern Africa and the Iberian Peninsula," *Economic Botany* 57, no. 4 (2003): 502–14.

"settlers from Europe planted citrus": Karen Ordahl Kupperman, "The Puzzle of the American Climate in the Early Colonial Period," *The American Historical Review* 87, no. 5 (1982): 1262–89; Sam White, "Unpuzzling American Climate: New World Experience and the Foundations of a New Science," *Isis* 106, no. 3 (2015): 544–66; Warren, "'Nature's Navels,'" 180.

"yields of the fruit increased forty-three times": Warren, 185.

"the first formalised citrus breeding programme": Iqrar A. Khan and Walter J. Kender, "Citrus Breeding: Introduction and Objectives," in *Citrus Genetics, Breeding, and Biotechnology*, ed. Iqrar A. Khan (Wallingford: CABI, 2007), 3.

"had never seen an orange tree before": W. C. Cooper, P. C. Reece, and J. R. Furr, "Citrus Breeding in Florida—Past, Present and Future," *Proceedings of the Florida State Horticultural Society* 75 (1962), 5–12.

"Swingle would guide the acquisition of East Asian texts": Walter T. Swingle, "Chinese Historical Sources," *The American Historical Review* 26, no. 4 (1921): 717–25; Hartmut Walravens, "Namen- und Titelregister zu den Jahresberichten über ostasiatische Neuerwerbungen der Library of Congress, Washington, D.C., 1912–1941," *Monumenta Serica* 69, no. 1 (2021): 201–41.

"Swingle described the tangelo in sensuous terms": Walter T. Swingle, T. Ralph Robinson, and E. M. Savage, "New Citrus Hybrids," *USDA Circular* 181 (August 1931): 7.

"Originally, it was named huáng*lung*bing": X. Y. Zhao, "Citrus Yellow Shoot (Huanglongbing) in China: A Review," *Proceedings of the International Society of Citriculture* 1 (1982): 466–69.

"Its impact is felt in citrus-producing regions": Cici Zhang, "Citrus Greening Is Killing the World's Orange Trees. Scientists Are Racing to Help," *Chemical and Engineering News* 97, no. 23 (2019).

"Saraiva traced clones of California oranges": Barbara Hahn, Tiago Saraiva, Paul W. Rhode, Peter Coclanis, and Claire Strom, "Does Crop Determine Culture?," *Agricultural History* 88, no. 3 (2014): 407–39.

"a history of Florida citrus": T. Ralph Robinson, "Some Aspects of the History of Citrus in Florida," *Quarterly Journal of the Florida Academy of Sciences* 8, no. 1 (1945): 65.

"three Florida citrus producers were sentenced to prison": Adrian Sainz, "Slavery in Florida's Citrus Groves," *CBS News*, November 21, 2002.

"it reached lows not seen since the 1940s": Abby Narishkin, Dylan Bank, Victoria Barranco, and Yin Liao, "After the Worst Orange Harvest in 75 Years, Florida Growers Are Trying to

Combat a Deadly Citrus Disease," *Business Insider,* May 18, 2022. www.businessinsider.com/florida-orange-growers-are -battling-deadly-citrus-disease-2022-5.

"it is tolerant to huánglóngbìng": Zhang, "Citrus Greening Is Killing the World's Orange Trees."

"they tried diversifying by planting bamboo": ABC7 Staff, "Mixon Fruit Farms Planning to Sell Remaining Land," ABC 7, October 25, 2022. www.mysuncoast.com/2022/10/25 /mixon-fruit-farms-planning-sell-remaining-land/; Dale White, "Mixon Fruit Farms Experimenting with Edible Organic Bamboo," *Sarasota Herald Tribune,* July 23, 2018. heraldtribune.com /story/news/local/manatee/2018/07/23/mixon-fruit-farms-experi menting-with-edible-organic-bamboo/11408585007/.

"given its botanical name by one Walter Tennyson Swingle": Walter T. Swingle, "A New Genus, Fortunella, Comprising Four Species of Kumquat Oranges," *Journal of the Washington Academy of Sciences* 5, no. 5 (1915): 165–76.

11. At the Scale of Water Drops

"the ways one might see a mushroom as kin": Anna Tsing, "Arts of Inclusion, or How to Love a Mushroom," *Manoa* 22, no. 2 (2010): 191–203.

"found in the east of Germany": Maren Hübers and Hans Kerp, "Oldest Known Mosses Discovered in Mississippian (Late Visean) Strata of Germany," *Geology* 40, no. 8 (2012): 755–58.

"a more-than-1,500-year-old *Chorisodontium aciphyllum* moss": Esme Roads, Royce E. Longton, and Peter Convey, "Millennial Timescale Regeneration in a Moss from Antarctica," *Current Biology* 24, no. 6 (2014): R222-R223.

"First described in 1801 by Johann Hedwig": Johann Hedwig, *Species Muscorum Frondosorum* (Leipzig: Barth, 1801), 147.

"hadn't been recorded in Britain in its sporulating stage": P. W. Richards, "*Campylopus introflexus* (Hedw.) Brid. and *C. polytrichoides* De Not. in the British Isles; a Preliminary Account," *Transactions of the British Bryological Society* 4, no. 3 (1963): 404–17.

"tank moss": Dr. Uwe Starfinger & Prof. Dr. Ingo Kowarik, "*Campylopus introflexus*," Neobiota.de (Bundesamt für Naturschutz), 2003. neobiota.bfn.de/handbuch/gefaesspflanzen /campylopus-introflexus.html.

"Its current nonnative range": Benjamin E. Carter, "Ecology and Distribution of the Introduced Moss Campylopus Introflexus (Dicranaceae) in Western North America," *Madroño* 61, no. 1 (2014): 82–86.

"could not compete where the heath star moss took hold": L. B. Sparrius and A. M. Kooijman, "Invasiveness of *Campylopus introflexus* in Drift Sands Depends on Nitrogen Deposition and Soil Organic Matter," *Applied Vegetation Science* 14 (2011): 221–29; Miguel Equihua and Michael B. Usher, "Impact of Carpets of the Invasive Moss *Campylopus introflexus* on Calluna Vulgaris Regeneration," *Journal of Ecology* 81, no. 2 (1993): 359–65.

"occurrences of the species across Great Britain": National Biodiversity Network Atlas. nbnatlas.org.

"'beautifully adapted for life in miniature'": Robin Wall Kimmerer, *Gathering Moss: A Natural and Cultural History of Mosses* (Corvallis: Oregon State University Press, 2003), 15.

"tiny microclimate in which a moss exists": Kimmerer, 16–18.

"'designed at the scale of water drops'": Alie Ward (host), "Episode 149: Bryology (MOSS) with Dr. Robin Wall Kimmerer," *Ologies* (podcast), June 30, 2020. www.alieward.com/ologies /bryology.

"a carpet of heath star moss is there and thickening": Starfinger and Kowarik, *"Campylopus introflexus"*; T. Hasse, "Campylopus introflexus," Cabi Compendium, Cabi International, 2022; Jonas Klinck, *"Campylopus introflexus,"* Nobanis Invasive Alien Species Fact Sheet, Online Database of the European Network on Invasive Alien Species, 2010.

"one account lays blame for the decline of the tawny pipit": Chris van Turnhout, "The Disappearance of the Tawny Pipit *Anthus campestris* as a Breeding Bird from the Netherlands and Northwest-Europe," (originally: "Het verdwijnen van de Duinpieper als broedvogel uit Nederland en Noordwest-Europa"), *Limosa* 78 (2005): 1–14.

"mosses experience the world as individual stems": Kimmerer, *Gathering Moss*, 77.

12. Seed

"an essential component of care for genetic material": Helen Anne Curry, "Data, Duplication, and Decentralisation: Gene Bank Management in the 1980s and 1990s," in *Towards Responsible Plant Data Linkage: Data Challenges for Agricultural Research and Development*, eds. Hugh F. Williamson and Sabina Leonelli (Cham: Springer, 2003), 163–82.

"'the ultimate insurance policy for the world's food supply'": Crop Trust, "Svalbard Global Seed Vault," 2022. www.croptrust .org/work/svalbard-global-seed-vault/.

"'the backup of the backup'": Helen Anne Curry, "The History of Seed Banking and the Hazards of Backup," *Social Studies of Science* 52, no. 5 (2022): 664–88.

"seen in contrast to the historic legacy of the Botanic Garden": Xan Sarah Chacko, "Digging Up Colonial Roots:

The Less-Known Origins of the Millennium Seed Bank Partnership," *Catalyst: Feminism, Theory, Technoscience* 5, no. 2 (2009): 1–9.

"makes banked seeds less useful in a changing world": Lauren Leffer, "Climate Change Is Shifting How Plants Evolve. Seed Banks May Have to Adapt, Too," *Gizmodo*, July 1, 2022. gizmodo.com/seed-banks-climate-change-food-security-sval bard-vault-1849073024.

"'a site from which to restore copies'": Curry, "The History of Seed Banking," 666.

"'seed determinists'": Francesca Bray, Barbara Hahn, John Bosco Lourdusamy, and Tiago Saraiva, "Cropscapes and History: Reflections on Rootedness and Mobility," *Transfers: Interdisciplinary Journal of Mobility Studies* 9, no. 1 (2019): 26; Can Dalyan, "Latent Capital: Seed Banking as Investment in Climate Change Futures," in *The Work That Plants Do: Life, Labour and the Future of Vegetal Economies*, eds. Marion Ernwein, Franklin Ginn, and James Palmer (Bielefeld: transcript Verlag, 2021), 189.

"both individual care and attention": Xan Sarah Chacko, "Creative Practices of Care: The Subjectivity, Agency, and Affective Labor of Preparing Seeds for Long-term Banking," *Culture, Agriculture, Food, and Environment* 41, no. 2 (2019): 97–106.

"asks about the nature of hope": Catriona Sandilands, "Fields of Dreams," *Resilience: A Journal of the Environmental Humanities* 4, no. 2–3 (2017): 113.

13. Pinetum

"He offered *Pinus mundayi* as their Latin binomial": Personal correspondence with Howard Falcon-Lang, November 24, 2022.

"the oldest known examples of a pine tree in history": Howard J. Falcon-Lang, Viola Mages, Margaret Collinson, "The Oldest *Pinus* and Its Preservation by Fire," *Geology* 44, no. 4 (2016): 303–306.

"pines are also especially helpful for understanding invasions": David M. Richardson, "*Pinus*: A Model Group for Unlocking the Secrets of Alien Plant Invasions?," *Preslia* 78 (2006): 376.

"Caspar David Friedrich's *Der Chasseur im Wald*": Simon Schama, *Landscape and Memory* (New York: Knopf, 1995), plate 13.

"we can therefore tell different kinds of stories": Sara Maitland, *Gossip from the Forest: The Tangled Roots of Our Forests and Fairytales* (London: Granta, 2012).

"he included an etching of the species": J. F. Arnold, *Reise nach Mariazell in Steyermark* (Vienna: Christian Friedrich Wappler, 1785), 8, 25.

"the Corsican pine had been introduced as early as 1759": Monty Don, "A Pine Romance," *The Guardian*, November 9, 2003. www.theguardian.com/lifeandstyle/2003/nov/09/gardens.

"a 'prejudice against Corsican timber'": Forestry Commission, *History of Thetford, King's, Swaffam Forests, 1923–1951* (Forestry Commission, 1952), 1.

"a map of pine distribution shows": Wei-Tao Jin, David S. Gernandt, Christian Wehenkel, Xiao-Mei Xia, Xiao-Xin Wei, and Xiao-Quan Wang, "Phylogenomic and Ecological Analyses Reveal the Spatiotemporal Evolution of Global Pines," *PNAS* 118, no. 20 (2021): e2022302118.

"Researchers believe these species to be southward migrants": Jin et al.

"the roots of Taiwanese red pine work to restore integrity to the mountainside": Liang-Chi Wang, Zih-Wei Tang, Huei-Fen Chen, Hong-Chun Li, Liang-Jian Shiau, Jyh-Jaan Steven Huang, Kuo-Yen Wei, Chih-Kai Chuang, and Yu-Min Chou, "Late Holocene Vegetation, Climate, and Natural Disturbance Records from an Alpine Pond in Central Taiwan," *Quaternary International* 528 (2019): 63–72; Wen-Chieh Chou, Wen-Tzu Lin, and Chao-Yuan Lin, "Vegetation Recovery Patterns Assessment at Landslides Caused by Catastrophic Earthquake: A Case Study in Central Taiwan," *Environ Monit Assess* 52 (2009): 245–57.

14. Synonyms for "Mauve"

"the lens of literature we are assigned in high school": Charlotte Brontë, *Jane Eyre* (London: Penguin Classics, 1996 [1847]), 370; Emily Brontë, *Wuthering Heights* (London: Hamish Hamilton, 1950 [1847]), 134.

"Anne is rapturous at the beauty of it": L. M. Montgomery, *Anne of the Island* (Toronto: George G. Harrap and Co. Ltd., 1938 [1915]), 62–63.

"a botanist named George Lawson tried to explain": George Lawson, "Notes on Some Nova Scotian Plants," *Proceedings and Transactions of the Nova Scotian Institute of Natural Science* 4, no. 2 (1876): 167–79.

"many reports on heather from the time": Asa Grey, "American Heather," *American Journal of Science* s2-43, no. 127 (1867): 128–29 [a short note in the section titled "Scientific Intelligence"]; Edward S. Rand Jr., "The Heather (*Calluna vulgaris*), a Native of the United States: Extracted from an Unpublished Report to the Massachusetts Horticultural Society," *American Journal of Science* s2-33, no. 97 (1862): 22–27.

"a 1958 round-up of heather research": Roy B. Clarkson, "Scotch Heather in North America," *Castanea* 23, no. 4 (1958): 119–30. www.jstor.org/stable/4031792.

"Powles writes of moving to England after a childhood in New Zealand": Nina Mingya Powles, "Small Bodies of Water," *The Willowherb Review*, no. 1 (2018). www.thewillowherbreview.com/bodies-of-water-nina-mingya-powles.

"my favourite cultural critic on nature": Raymond Williams, *The Country and the City* (New York: Oxford University Press, 1975 [1973]), 258.

"a modest array of plants over two visits to Hampstead Heath": Thomas Johnson, *Botanical Journeys in Kent and Hampstead: A facsimile reprint with Introduction and Translation of his Iter Plantarum 1629, Descriptio Itineris Plantarum 1632*, ed. J. S. L. Gilmour (Pittsburgh: Hunt Botanical Library, 1972).

"Eversley specifically mourns the loss of heather": Lord Eversley (George Shaw Lefevre), *Commons, Forests & Footpaths: The Story of the Battle During the Last Forty-Five Years for Public Rights Over the Commons, Forests and Footpaths of England and Wales* (London: Cassell, 1910), 34–35.

"a 'true heath'": Hampstead Scientific Society, *Hampstead Heath: Its Geology and Natural History* (London: T. Fisher Unwin, 1913), 105.

"On a map of ancient Mediterranean 'purple-producing sites'": Chris Cooksey, "Tyrian Purple: The First Four Thousand Years," *Science Progress* 96, no. 2 (2013): 171–86.

"encyclopaedia entries on 'purple'": "Purple," *Encyclopædia Britannica*, September 8, 2020. www.britannica.com/science/purple-colour.

"photographs of the land here at the time": Walter Peters, *40 Jahre Schneverdingen 1946–1986. Fakten, Daten, Bilder. Eine Dokumentation* (Schneverdingen: Stadt Schneverdingen, 1987), 278–82.

"the site's heathland habitat was painstakingly restored": "Schneverdingen: Naturschutzgebiet Osterheide," Lüneburger Heide GmbH Website, accessed October 6, 2022. www.luene burger-heide.de/natur/sehenswuerdigkeit/574/schneverdingen -osterheide-naturschutz.html.

JESSICA J. LEE is a British Canadian Taiwanese author, environmental historian, and winner of the Hilary Weston Writers' Trust Prize for Nonfiction, the Boardman Tasker Award for Mountain Literature, the Banff Mountain Book Award, and the RBC Taylor Prize Emerging Writer Award. She is the author of *Turning*, *Two Trees Make a Forest*, and the children's book *A Garden Called Home*, and co-editor of the essay collection *Dog Hearted*. She is the founding editor of *The Willowherb Review* and teaches creative writing at the University of Cambridge. She lives in Berlin.